"Embracing a robust theology framed in th[e] ... fall, redemption, and consummation, Jim H[...] tural texts, displaying how human work is a central thread in the biblical storyline. No matter the present depth of the reader's understanding of the integration of faith and work, the insights gained will prove inspiring and transformational."

Tom Nelson, author, *Work Matters;* Senior Pastor, Christ Community Church; President, Made to Flourish

"The Bible has much more to say about work than we often think! Hamilton shows us just how central work is to the biblical storyline and God's plan to fill the earth with his glory. This is a profound book that dives deep into the Scriptures yet remains highly accessible. There are surprising insights on almost every page. This is now one of the best books on the biblical view of work today."

Matt Perman, Director of Marketing, Made to Flourish; author, *What's Best Next: How the Gospel Transforms the Way You Get Things Done*

"People's lives get turned upside down when they realize God cares intensely about their daily work. This short book walks us step by step through the big story of the Bible to show that God's purpose for our daily labor is one of Scripture's deepest and most important themes."

Greg Forster, Director, Oikonomia Network, Trinity International University

"If you want to fully grasp the depth of the biblical theology of work, you will not be disappointed by James Hamilton's short but powerful book. As he walks you through the biblical narrative of creation, fall, redemption, and restoration, you will develop a deeper appreciation of God's plan for his redeemed images to truly flourish, both in this world and the world to come."

Hugh Whelchel, Executive Director, Institute for Faith, Work & Economics; author, *How Then Should We Work? Rediscovering the Biblical Doctrine of Work*

"There is no shortage of quality books on the connection between faith and work. But James Hamilton's *Work and Our Labor in the Lord* is in a class all its own: a thorough, yet concise, examination of the place of work in biblical theology. This is a must-read for all Christians."

Joe Carter, Editor, The Gospel Coalition; contributor, *NIV Lifehacks Bible*

"This book may be short, but it is extremely rich. Hamilton is a surefooted guide to the scriptural material and provides a highly valuable and stimulating discussion of the entire sweep of the biblical theology of work."

Gary Millar, author, *Now Choose Life: Theology and Ethics in Deuteronomy*; *Saving Eutychus*; and *Calling on the Name of the Lord*

Work and Our Labor in the Lord

Other Crossway books in the Short Studies
in Biblical Theology Series

Marriage and the Mystery of the Gospel, Ray Ortlund (2016)

The Son of God and the New Creation, Graeme Goldsworthy (2015)

Work and Our Labor in the Lord

James M. Hamilton Jr.

Dane C. Ortlund and Miles V. Van Pelt,
series editors

WHEATON, ILLINOIS

Trade paperback ISBN: 978-1-4335-4995-3
epub ISBN: 978-1-4335-4998-4
PDF ISBN: 978-1-4335-4996-0
Mobipocket ISBN: 978-1-4335-4997-7

Library of Congress Cataloging-in-Publication Data

Names: Hamilton, James M., 1974- author.
Title: Work and our labor in the Lord / James M. Hamilton Jr.
Description: Wheaton, Illinois : Crossway, 2017. | Series: Short studies in biblical theology series | Includes bibliographical references and index.
Identifiers: LCCN 2016027439 (print) | LCCN 2016033561 (ebook) | ISBN 9781433549953 (tp) | ISBN 978433549984 (epub) | ISBN 978143349960 (pdf) | ISBN 9781433549977 (mobi)
Subjects: LCSH: Work—Religious aspects—Christianity. | Work—Biblical teaching.
Classification: LCC BT738.5 .H355 2017 (print) | LCC BT738.5 (ebook) | DDC 261.8/5—dc23
LC record available at https://lccn.loc.gov/2016027439

Crossway is a publishing ministry of Good News Publishers.

BP		27	26	25	24	23	22	21	20	19	18	17
15	14	13	12	11	10	9	8	7	6	5	4	3	2	1

For Kameron Slater,
a blessing to all who know him

Contents

Introduction

How did the biblical authors view work? To answer this question we need to understand the place of work in biblical theology. Biblical theology, in my view, is the attempt to understand and embrace the interpretive perspective of the biblical authors.[1] To attempt to understand the interpretive perspective of the biblical authors is to attempt to understand their *worldview*. The only access we have to their worldview is what they wrote. Understanding the worldview of the biblical authors requires the ability to see the ways they intended their statements to be read against a wider understanding of the *history of redemption*, and I am convinced that an evangelical and canonical approach to these issues best positions us to make progress in the task of understanding and embracing the interpretive perspective of the biblical authors.[2] One's perspective on redemptive history will be an inextricable component of one's worldview, and if we are pursuing *biblical* theology we will (whether consciously or not) oper-

---

1. James M. Hamilton Jr., *What Is Biblical Theology?* (Wheaton, IL: Crossway, 2014).

2. Those who have read Edward W. Klink and Darian R. Lockett, *Understanding Biblical Theology: A Comparison of Theory and Practice* (Grand Rapids, MI: Zondervan, 2012) will see that I am consciously combining what they describe as three different types of biblical theology (history of redemption, worldview story, and canonical approach). In my view, these issues are inseparable. I have attempted biblical theology in this way in *God's Glory in Salvation through Judgment: A Biblical Theology* (Wheaton, IL: Crossway, 2010); and *With the Clouds of Heaven: The Book of Daniel in Biblical Theology*, New Studies in Biblical Theology (Downers Grove, IL: IVP Academic, 2014).

ate with some kind of perspective on the relationships between the various books of the Bible.

Because this is a biblical theological study of the topic of work, the structure of the canon will play a less explicit role.[3] For our purposes here, the following questions will help us to seek the interpretive perspective of the biblical authors on the topic of work:

- What part did work play in the big story of the world through which the biblical authors interpreted their lives?
- What propositional truths about work did they understand to flow out of and back into that big story?
- Do the biblical authors understand work to symbolize something beyond mere labor?

These questions will be used to get at what the biblical authors believed about work, and when we have understood what they believed about work, we will know what we should believe about it.

We will begin with (1) God's design for work in the very good creation, prior to sin. From there we will move to consider (2) what work looks like in a fallen world, (3) what work should be in the kingdom that the Lord Christ has inaugurated, and finally (4) what the Bible indicates about work in the new heaven and the new earth the Lord Jesus will bring. We will thus look at work at creation, after the fall, now that Christ has accomplished redemption, and in the restoration.

A word about biblical theological method: on the one hand, the contents of this book move through the salvation-historical storyline, i.e., the worldview story of creation-fall-redemption-restoration. On

---

3. For further discussion, see Stephen G. Dempster, *Dominion and Dynasty: A Biblical Theology of the Hebrew Bible*, New Studies in Biblical Theology (Downers Grove, IL: IVP Academic, 2003), 15–51; and for a comprehensive consideration of the issues, see Roger T. Beckwith, *The Old Testament Canon of the New Testament Church and Its Background in Early Judaism* (Grand Rapids, MI: Eerdmans, 1985).

the other hand, in chapters 2 (fall/old-covenant instructions) and 3 (redemption/new-covenant instructions) we are not looking at *events* that can be plotted on the storyline but considering the gracious instructions God gave to his people for everyday life.

The incorporation of Old Testament Wisdom Literature into biblical theology has sometimes been seen as a challenge, particularly for those who move along the salvation-historical storyline, as this study does. Chapter 2 gives considerable attention to the ways that the books of Ecclesiastes and Proverbs speak to work in everyday life under the old covenant, so here the Wisdom Literature is having its biblical theological say.[4]

We are looking for the interpretive perspective of the biblical authors. The following four chapters will enable us to explore work as it was meant to be, as it is, as it can be, and as it will be.

---

4. A longer project could include discussion of the Song of Solomon, particularly in light of what we will see about marriage and work in chapter 1. Time and space do not permit such discussion here, but see James M. Hamilton Jr., *Song of Songs: A Biblical-Theological, Allegorical, Christological Interpretation* (Fearn, UK: Christian Focus, 2015).

1

Creation

Work in the Very Good Garden

The stories we tell reveal our understanding of the world, with our hopes and fears, and the songs we sing are poetic crystallizations of the deep longings of our hearts. The deep longings of our hearts correspond to what we envision as the good life. Our vision of the good life can be understood as our vision of "the kingdom."[1]

God's Design for Work

The soundtrack to the movie *O Brother, Where Art Thou?* includes the song "Big Rock Candy Mountain."[2] The lyrics celebrate handouts that grow on bushes, trees that sprout cigarettes, and bulldogs that have rubber teeth so their watchdog bites are harmless. This song's idyllic landscape includes streams of alcohol beside a lake of stew,

---

1. See further James K. A. Smith, *Desiring the Kingdom: Worship, Worldview, and Cultural Formation* (Grand Rapids, MI: Baker Academic, 2009).
2. First recorded by Harry McClintock in 1928.

and whiskey too, because those who sing it want to escape reality by means of intoxication and to be fed though they have not worked. They want mountains made of rock candy. They want no tools such as shovels, axes, saws, or picks. They want to sleep all day, and they want to hang the jerk that invented work. I wonder if the songwriter realized that would put the noose around God's neck!

The song's sentiments fall significantly short of the glory that God intended when he created man in his own image and gave him work to do. Life at the Big Rock Candy Mountain would not result in true and lasting happiness or satisfaction. The Bible says there is a primal mountain that is our destination, but it's not one that will rot teeth and indulge character deficiencies. Contrast "Big Rock Candy Mountain" with Psalm 128:

> A Song of Ascents.
>
> Blessed is everyone who fears the LORD,
>   who walks in his ways!
> You shall eat the fruit of the labor of your hands;
>   you shall be blessed, and it shall be well with you.
> Your wife will be like a fruitful vine
>   within your house;
> your children will be like olive shoots
>   around your table.
> Behold, thus shall the man be blessed
>   who fears the LORD.
> The LORD bless you from Zion!
>   May you see the prosperity of Jerusalem all the days of
>   your life!
> May you see your children's children!
>   Peace be upon Israel!

This song is addressed to a man who works, and the blessing comes to him because he fears Yahweh and walks in Yahweh's ways. The blessing of Yahweh takes the form of this man enjoying the results of his work, which he has done to provide for his wife and children. Psalm 128's depiction of the good life, then, entails hard work done to provide for others, dependents, whose growth and fruitfulness are evidence of God's favor and blessing. Prosperity here includes godliness, responsibility, stewardship, and awareness of God, prompting fear and obedience and virtue.

The man blessed in Psalm 128 is a God-fearing man (v. 4), and in the context of the whole book of Psalms, the mention of Zion in verse 5 evokes the Davidic king Yahweh set there (cf. Ps. 2:6).[3] The references to the prosperity of Jerusalem and children and grandchildren in verses 5 and 6 hint that what has resulted in this individual blessed man experiencing the joys of Psalm 128 has spread to the wider culture. Jerusalem prospers because its men fear God, obey his Word, and work with their hands for the benefit of their wives and children. Psalm 128 is a poetic depiction of the blessings of the Mosaic covenant (cf. Leviticus 26 and Deuteronomy 28).

"Big Rock Candy Mountain" and Psalm 128 sing different versions of the good life. In the Bible, the land of promise is not the place sought by freeloaders and slackers who long for an El Dorado where theft is easy, the hills are made of sugar, work is abolished, and handouts are freely distributed to tramps and bums who have neither responsibilities nor families.

The Bible's songs are rooted in hopes seeded by its wider story, watered by God's promises. What is the role of work in that story? We begin our answer to that question by looking at what God created

---

3. For the significance of Psalms 1–2 for the whole book of Psalms, see Robert L. Cole, *Psalms 1–2: Gateway to the Psalter* (Sheffield, UK: Sheffield Phoenix Press, 2013); see also Gordon J. Wenham, *The Psalter Reclaimed: Praying and Praising with the Psalms* (Wheaton, IL: Crossway, 2013).

the good life to look like, when the world was without sin. We will start with work in the garden in Genesis 1–2. From there we will seek insight on what life in Eden could have been like from the blessings of the covenant in Deuteronomy 28:1–14. We will then consider how the judgment on God-given tasks in Genesis 3:16–19 subjects work to futility (cf. Rom. 8:20).

Work in the Garden (Genesis 1–2)

The Bible's story of the world opens with God doing work, six days of it. Once completed, not from weariness but because the work was done, God rested on the seventh day (Gen. 1:1–2:3; Heb. 4:3–4). Given that man is made in God's image and likeness (Gen. 1:27), with Christians called to be imitators of God (Eph. 5:1), the fact that the Bible opens with this scene of God doing the work of creation by his powerful word calls for reflection. God works by speaking words. Among other things, this validates all kinds of knowledge work in which the hard work of thinking and communicating accomplishes what those made in God's image have set out to do. But what words are like God's words? What words could make worlds?

In addition to being able to marshal his army of words to accomplish his purposes, then, we see from this vast and splendid universe that God is a skilled worker who completes his tasks with unparalleled excellence and creativity. Work is neither punishment nor cursed drudgery but an exalted, Godlike activity. Nor should we think that once God completed the work of creation he was finished with work—as though he made the watch then simply left it to tick away the seconds. As a justification for his right to heal on the Sabbath, Jesus declared, "My Father is working until now, and I am working" (John 5:17). The Bible opens with a depiction of God at work, and the operational understanding throughout the Bible is that God continues to work, guiding, upholding, loving, judging, and saving.

The first thing the Bible shows us about God is that he is a creative, competent, efficient, caring worker, whose work provides for others, blesses others, meets the needs of others, and makes life possible for them. Surely this is meant to inform readers of Genesis as they confront the idea of man made male and female in the image and likeness of God (Gen. 1:26–28).[4]

The creation of man and woman is accompanied by a blessing and a task, a charge and commission, which spring from God's intention for man as he made them, male and female. Genesis 1:26 presents God intending to grant *dominion*, royal rule, over the animal kingdom from the moment he decides to make man in his own image and likeness—indeed, dominion *because* made in God's image and likeness. God made male and female in his own image (Gen. 1:27); then he blessed them and told them what he wanted them to do (1:28).

Man was created not for passive observation of the world but for an epic task, a worldwide venture. Genesis 1:28 recounts,

> And God blessed them. And God said to them, "Be fruitful and multiply and fill the earth and subdue it, and have dominion over the fish of the sea and over the birds of the heavens and over every living thing that moves on the earth."

God commands the man and woman in Genesis 1:28 to be fruitful and multiply and thereby fill the earth—the whole thing. Then they are to subdue it—the whole thing. God next charges them to exercise dominion over the animal kingdom—the whole thing. The tasks in Genesis 1:28 are interrelated and interdependent. Man is to be

---

4. On this theme, see now Richard Lints, *Identity and Idolatry: The Image of God and Its Inversion*, New Studies in Biblical Theology (Downers Grove, IL: IVP Academic, 2015).

fruitful and multiply so as to fill, subdue, and rule. It is interesting to observe that in order to subdue and rule, man will have to be fruitful, multiply, and fill. This makes the fact that man was made male and female (1:27) indispensable.[5]

The marriage of the man and the woman (Gen. 2:18–25) will make possible the fruitful multiplication, which will enable the filling, subduing, and ruling. This tells us that the work God gave the man to do is not to be disconnected from marriage and family. In fact, marriage and family enable the man to accomplish the work God told him to do. These foundational realities in Genesis naturally give rise to songs such as Psalm 128, where the blessed man enjoys the fruits of his labor in the context of his family.

In the very good world as God created it (Gen. 1:31), prior to the entrance of sin (cf. 3:1–8), God gave man marriage to enable the completion of God-given and God-sized responsibilities. This is true in merely logistical terms—without the woman the man cannot be fruitful, multiply, and fill the earth. What the narrative draws our attention to, however, is the more significant relational blessing that God's gift of the woman was designed to be.[6] God said that it was not good for the man to be alone (Gen. 2:18), and he created a very good companion in the woman (2:22). This means that the fellowship and companionship and soul-deep oneness in the marriage of the man and the woman (2:23–25) were given to make the filling, subduing, and ruling over the world a delightful adventure undertaken together.

In the true story Genesis tells, God gave marriage not only to

---

5. For the vital necessity of women and motherhood, see my essay, "A Biblical Theology of Motherhood," *Journal of Discipleship and Family Ministry* 2, no. 2 (2012): 6–13.

6. Contrast this with the Greek myth that purports to explain the creation of women as punishment for men in the poem "Works and Days" by Hesiod, *The Homeric Hymns and Homerica*, trans. Hugh G. Evelyn-White, Loeb Classical Library 57 (Cambridge, MA: Harvard University Press, 1914), 7.

enable the great task but also to *enrich* the life and work God gave to man.

Again, the multiplying is for filling, and the filling is for the image of God to cover the dry lands as the waters cover the seas so that all the earth will be subdued by those who image forth God's likeness, and thus all animals will be ruled by those who exercise godly dominion. The subduing of the earth seems to call for wild tangles of vegetation to be transformed into places where humans can live and cultivate gardens. The dominion over the animals suggests a stewardship of all living creatures so that all enjoy God's goodness.

To summarize: God built a cosmic temple when he called creation into being.[7] In that temple he placed his own image and likeness. He then blessed his image and likeness and charged them with a responsibility. Their job was to make the world that God made good (Gen. 1:31) even better (!) for both plant and animal life. Being in God's image and likeness, mankind was to cultivate the world of vegetation and living creatures in ways reflecting God's own character and creativity.

Humans were made and put on earth as the visible representations of the character, authority, and rule of the invisible God.

A fundamental answer to the question of why we are here, therefore, is that we are here to reflect the character of God in the way we subdue the earth and exercise dominion over the animal kingdom under the blessing of God. Doing these things as the image and likeness of God means that our task is to bring the nature and character of God to bear on all living things in the world that God made.[8]

Work is therefore built into the created order, right from the start. God gave man stewardship of the land and all life on it. All tasks man

---

7. G. K. Beale, *The Temple and the Church's Mission: A Biblical Theology of the Dwelling Place of God*, New Studies in Biblical Theology (Downers Grove, IL: IVP Academic, 2004).

8. So also Lints, *Identity and Idolatry*, 56.

undertakes in God's world can be seen in relationship to that original commission. Some jobs deal directly with plants and animals. Other jobs enable the stewardship of land and life. All jobs relate to those great tasks. The making of roads and markets enables us to subdue the earth and exercise dominion over the animals. The tasks related to helping other humans to flourish intellectually and spiritually enable people to deal with the land and living creatures. Arguably every righteous task in the world—from that of the farmer or rancher to that of the engineer, the software developer, or the nuclear physicist, from that of the ditchdigger to the physician (or veterinarian), from the coach to the pastor, the zookeeper to the politician, the sergeant to the mailman—every task in the world can be seen in relationship to the subjection of the earth and the exercise of dominion over the animal kingdom.

Not all jobs are righteous, of course. Sometimes wicked people hire others to commit sin: people are paid to commit murder, to bear false witness, to corrupt justice, or to commit adultery. Such jobs not only transgress God's commands; they image forth the character of the usurper rather than the likeness of the Creator.

At its most basic level, a righteous job is one that does not exist to commit or promote sin but to accomplish the tasks God gave to humanity at the beginning: fill, subdue, rule. Such work affords everyone who does it the opportunity to image forth the likeness of the one living and true God.

Genesis 1:26–28 tells us who we are as human beings and what God put us here to do. Who we are as the bearers of the image and likeness of the Creator is inherent in what God has given us to do. The filling, subduing, and ruling are to be done for God's sake and in God's way to display God's own character. There is to be no disconnect between what a man is and the way he does his work. How a man understands himself, his fundamental assumptions about the world, God, and his own sense of purpose will be made manifest in the way he does his work.

We get more insight into what God made man and woman to do in the Genesis 2 interpretive expansion on the Genesis 1 creation narrative. The connection between man and the working of the land can be seen in Genesis 2:5: "When no bush of the field was yet in the land and no small plant of the field had yet sprung up—for the LORD God had not caused it to rain on the land, and there was no man to work the ground . . ." Here Moses is not directly discussing man's role, but man's function is clear from the explanatory comment that God had not yet made man, so there was not yet a man to work the ground. This unexplored explanatory comment shows that Moses assumes that his audience will understand what he declares in the near context (e.g., 1:28; 2:15): that man was made to exercise stewardship over God's world by working the land.

The idea that man was made to work the ground is elaborated upon in Genesis 2:15, which states, "And Yahweh God took the man and caused him to rest in the garden of Eden to work it and to keep it" (AT). This is the first instance in the Bible of the term I have rendered "rest" (נוח), but the root will appear again in the naming of Noah (נח) in Genesis 5:29, where Noah's father articulates the hope that Noah will be the seed of the woman who will roll back the curse on the land (cf. Gen. 3:17–19 and 5:29). Earlier in Genesis 2 a different term was used to describe the way God "rested" (שבת) from his work on the seventh day. When God completed his work, he took a Sabbath, as it were (our word *Sabbath* being derived from the verb used to describe God resting on the seventh day, *shabbat*). When God put man in the garden to work, by contrast, he caused him to rest (נוח) there. John Piper once said on a panel discussion, "Productivity is restful to my soul." God caused Adam to rest in the garden that he might work it and keep it. Genesis 2:15 seems to point to a restorative rhythm of work and rest, even a restful work.

Significant, too, is the fact that God put the man in the garden to work and keep it. This language, "work and keep," could also be rendered "guard and serve," and these terms are found together elsewhere in the Pentateuch only when they describe the duties of the Levites at the tabernacle, which they were to guard, where they were to minister (e.g., Num. 3:7–8).[9] Once Moses's audience has gotten as far as Numbers, subsequent encounters of the use of this language in Genesis 2:15 cast a priestly hue over the work that God put Adam in the garden to do.

God charged man with the tasks of filling, subduing, and ruling in Genesis 1:28, and this same task is restated as working and keeping the garden in Genesis 2:15. Working the garden (2:15), thus, elaborates on the charge to subdue the earth (1:28), even as the tasks of filling and subduing the earth indicate that the man and the woman were to work together to make all the land that God made like the garden of Eden. Keeping the garden (2:15) would seem to overlap with the exercise of dominion over fish, birds, and land animals (1:28). Fruits and flowers can be delicate things that need to be protected from the unwieldy bulk of an elephant or the overenthusiastic puppy. Given the fact that serpents and other animals will later be declared unclean,[10] the man's work of keeping the garden may have included the task of keeping snakes out (cf. Gen. 3:1).

The narrative of Genesis 2 proceeds to show God guiding the man through what it will look like for him to subdue the earth and exercise dominion over the animals. We also see what working and

---

9. See Gordon J. Wenham, "Sanctuary Symbolism in the Garden of Eden Story," in *I Studied Inscriptions from before the Flood : Ancient Near Eastern, Literary, and Linguistic Approaches to Genesis 1–11*, ed. Richard Hess and David Toshio Tsumara (Winona Lake, IN: Eisenbrauns, 1994), 399–404.

10. See Leviticus 11: for serpents v. 42; for lizards vv. 29–30.

keeping the garden entails, as the man is to keep *himself* from the forbidden Tree of the Knowledge of Good and Evil, on pain of death (2:17).

Reinforcing the interconnectedness of marriage and family with work, for the man cannot be fruitful and multiply by himself, God says that it is not good for the man to be alone. God then purposes to remedy what is not good by making a helper for the man (Gen. 2:18). Just as the man was made to work and keep the garden (2:15), the woman was made to help the man (2:18). These roles are built into the nature of man and woman by the one who created humanity male and female as his own image.

The man's role of working will entail providing; his role of keeping will entail protecting; and implicit in the narrative we also see that the man is to lead since he has heard the prohibition in Genesis 2:17 though the woman has not. The man was to provide, protect, and lead.

What does the woman's role of helping entail? Perhaps it would be easier to say what helping does not entail, for helping would seem to involve everything *but* what the man is to do. God created the woman so that together they could be fruitful and multiply, and God created her to help the man lead, protect, and provide. The jobs were given to the man to do, and the woman was given to help him do them. These roles are established so that together the man and the woman can accomplish the tasks set out in Genesis 1:28 and 2:15.

They can multiply only together. They cannot do that without a total investment in the project from both. They can fill the earth only with their children, and they can subdue the earth and have dominion over all those animals only with the help of those children. Clearly these children will need strong character and a diligent work ethic for the big jobs before them.

Our culture is in revolt against the idea that biology corresponds to sexual identity, to say nothing of the fact that some roles are given to men that are not given to women, and vice versa. The revolt seeks to overthrow the "gender binary," the view that humanity exists as male and female, as though being either biologically male or female is too restrictive a way to approach the issue.[11] Rather than viewing biological sex and the accompanying gender roles as some kind of straitjacket, however, we should receive how God made us as his gift and purpose for us and marvel at the enormous freedom and flexibility within the broad indications of God's created purpose for the man to work and keep and for the woman to help. The specifics are not spelled out, leaving room for different personalities and relationships to maneuver freely as they dance to the music.

The creational realities are like the ballroom, within which we find the dance floor, with the music and its beat provided as well. How each married couple dances to the music is up to them, but as creatures in God's world they will dance in this ballroom, on this dance floor, to this music, with the man leading and the woman helping. Not to do so is to rebel against the created order.

A theological analogy can be observed between the interpersonal relationships enjoyed by the members of the Trinity and the creation of male and female in the image of God (Gen. 1:27). Within the Godhead, among the members of the Trinity, we find that the Father takes on certain roles, the Son takes other roles, and the Spirit does other things also. There is a diversity of persons and responsibilities within the Trinity, and God creates humanity in his image and likeness of two sexes, male and female, with differing responsibilities. As Richard Lints writes of the plural ("let us") in Genesis 1:26, "The immediate context at least signals a reflection

---

11. For a full treatment of these issues, see Denny Burk, *What Is the Meaning of Sex?* (Wheaton, IL: Crossway, 2013).

of the Creator in human creatures. And that reflection must be considered relational in part."[12]

Men and women who reject the distinctions in roles given to male and female at creation rebel against God's purpose: he made man male and female to reflect his own image and likeness. We cannot reflect the character of God's unified diversity as the one God who ever exists as three persons if we reject the roles *he gave* to man and woman.

The world ranged against God has cultivated a sense that what is "normal" is for biological sex to be irrelevant both to gender identity and to the nature of the work someone does. In Genesis 1–2 by contrast, biological sex is directly tied to the roles given to man and woman. Our society is in rebellion against God's created order. This aspect of secular culture is at war with God's purpose for people as men and women. This culture also wants to normalize sexual rebellion, redefining marriage to include same-sex unions that by their very nature cannot be fruitful and multiply.[13]

The man exercises God's dominion over the animals by naming them (Gen. 2:19–20), and then the man names the woman (2:21–23). The man's exercise of his God-given authority over the woman, naming her, partakes of no oppression, no exploitation, and no lack of concern. It is noble, loving, biological, theological, true, righteous, pure, and poetic.

God built this vast world, and then he created two people whose responsibility it was to be fruitful and multiply and fill this world, to subdue the earth and to exercise dominion over all the animals. Can you imagine a bigger task? Could there be a more daunting challenge, a more ambitious undertaking?

---

12. Lints, *Identity and Idolatry*, 68.
13. See Sherif Girgis, Robert George, and Ryan T. Anderson, "What Is Marriage?," *Harvard Journal of Law and Public Policy* 34 (2010): 245–87; and Denny Burk and Heath Lambert, *Transforming Homosexuality: What the Bible Says about Sexual Orientation and Change* (Phillipsburg, NJ: P&R, 2015).

What does God do to enable the man and the woman to accomplish these tasks? He made them in his image and likeness and blessed them (Gen. 1:26–28), and he gave them to each other in marriage (2:22–24).

What Moses narrated in Genesis 2:22–23 prompted a statement in 2:24 that applies what just took place between the first man and woman to all humanity. In Matthew 19:4–5 Jesus says that the Creator spoke the words of Genesis 2:24. This means that on the basis of what happens in Genesis 2:18–23, God says that men are to leave their parents and cleave to a wife, the two becoming one flesh (cf. Matt. 19:4). Note that to this point in Genesis 1–2 neither the man nor the woman has a father or a mother, but God is speaking in 2:24 of a man leaving his father and mother. This assumes that from what takes place in this scene forward, all men everywhere will have a father and a mother. In fact it is impossible to have a male child, or any child, without a father and a mother. Those male children are to leave their parents, cleave to a wife, and become one flesh with her, and then the new pair becomes father and mother.

Before moving from this discussion of Genesis 1–2, let us return to our guiding questions in an attempt to bring together what we have observed to this point.

What role does work play in the Bible's big story? By charging the man to be fruitful and multiply and fill the earth and subdue it, having dominion over all other creatures, God was commanding his image bearers, the visible representation of the authority and character of the invisible God, to cover the dry lands with the glory of God as the waters cover the seas.[14] This means that at the root level, man's task is to work in such a way that from the rising of the sun to the place of its setting, the name of the Lord is praised, the goodness

---

14. Cf. Lints, *Identity and Idolatry*, 53: "creation is 'built' for worship."

of God is savored, and the character of God is known and enacted. Thus the work that Adam made impossible by his sin is the work that Jesus has made possible through his death and resurrection and will accomplish when he returns. The earth will indeed be full of the knowledge of the glory of the Lord.

What propositional truths about work flow out of and back into that big story? The task of multiplying and filling the earth so as to subdue it and have dominion over the animals makes marriage foundational to the work that God gave man and woman to do on the earth. From the pre-fall, pre-curse narrative in Genesis 1 and 2 Paul derives normative, prescriptive gender roles determined by biological sex. Paul bases his argument that men and women are to be distinguished from one another both in behavior and apparel on the reality that the woman was made from man and that the woman was created for the man (1 Cor. 11:8–9; cf. 11:2–16; 1 Tim. 2:9–15).[15] This means that so-called egalitarians have rejected the roles assigned to men and women by the Creator on the basis of biological sex. We can further say that same-sex "marriage" and transgenderism rebel against the created order by rejecting the normative nature of Genesis 1:27 and 2:24 articulated by Jesus in Matthew 19:4–5. Same-sex marriages cannot be fruitful and multiply, and transgender behavior rejects the sex assigned by the Creator.

On the positive side, we can say that the narratives present the man's job in the context of his family. Adam was to work the garden

---

15. For an exposition of 1 Corinthians 11, see James M. Hamilton Jr., "Gender Roles and the Glory of God: A Sermon on 1 Corinthians 11:2–12," *Journal for Biblical Manhood and Womanhood* 9 (2004): 35–39; on 1 Timothy 2, see Thomas R. Schreiner and Andreas J. Köstenberger, *Women in the Church: An Analysis and Application of 1 Timothy 2:9–15*, 2nd ed. (Grand Rapids, MI: Baker Academic, 2005); for a synthesis of the relevant NT passages, see James M. Hamilton Jr., "What Women Can Do in Ministry: Full Participation within Biblical Boundaries," in *Women, Ministry and the Gospel: Exploring New Paradigms* (Downers Grove, IL: IVP Academic, 2007), 32–52; and for discussion of virtually every aspect of the debate, see Wayne Grudem, *Evangelical Feminism and Biblical Truth: An Analysis of More Than 100 Disputed Questions* (Sisters, OR: Multnomah, 2004).

and protect it. He was to lead his wife and the brood they begat, provide for her and the children through his work, and protect his wife and offspring as he guarded the garden.

Does work point beyond mere labor? Being in the image and likeness of God, working to fill the earth with God's image bearers, subduing it according to God's character, ruling it as God's representative—work points to the character and glory of God. As man works, he is to make the ways of the invisible God visible to any and all who behold what he does.

Genesis 1–2 is the archetypal fountainhead of biblical symbolism, and it seems that the work spoken of in these chapters, working and keeping the garden, subduing the earth and exercising dominion over the creatures, symbolizes all the work that man will do under heaven.

We know what happens in Genesis 3. But can you imagine what life would be like had Adam not sinned? We can fertilize our imaginations on this point from the descriptions of the good life in the land that hint at what life and work were meant to be. These descriptions can be found, among other places, in texts such as Psalm 128 and the blessings of the covenant, where God promised what life would be if his people would obey his commands (see Lev. 26:1–13 and Deut. 28:1–14). We turn to a consideration of the blessings of the covenant for more light on what life under God's blessing was meant to be.

The Blessings of the Covenant (Deut. 28:1–14)

Why would the blessings of the covenant give insight into what unfallen life in Eden would have been like? Because though sin got Adam expelled from Eden, God did not alter his purpose from what he set out to achieve when he put Adam there in the first place. That purpose was and is to cover the dry lands with his glory. The promise made in Genesis 3:15 was passed down through the genealogies of Genesis 5 and 11, and then the blessing of Abraham in Genesis 12:1–3 elaborated upon the promise. That blessing of Abraham was passed to Isaac in Genesis 26:3 and to Jacob in 28:4. The blessing is then passed to the sons of Joseph in Genesis 48:15–20, but the blessing of Judah indicates that the conquering king would come from him (Gen. 49:8–12; cf. 1 Chron. 5:1–2).

The wording of Genesis 5:1–3 creates the impression that as Seth was Adam's son in his image and likeness, so, in a sense, Adam was God's son in his image and likeness (cf. Luke 3:38). Along these lines, when God declares that the nation of Israel is his firstborn son, it is as though the nation of Israel has become a new Adam. When God brings Israel into the Land of Promise, it is as though the new Adam enters the new Eden with a new opportunity to dwell in God's land under God's law enjoying God's blessing. Just as Adam was to expand the borders of the garden to fill the world with God's glory, so Israel's king was offered the ends of the earth as his possession (Ps. 2:8–9).

For Israel to enjoy the Land of Promise by keeping the Mosaic covenant would be for them to realize God's purposes and experience God's blessing. It would be as close to Eden as someone could get on this side of Adam's sin.

We will look mainly at Deuteronomy 28, but there is one element of Leviticus 26 that particularly corresponds to the scene in the garden of Eden: the presence of God. The best thing about life in Eden was that God walked there with man in the cool of the day (Gen. 3:8). The best thing about Israel's life in covenant with God was that God promised to make his dwelling among them (Lev. 26:11–13). Once this has been stated in Leviticus, it is assumed all through the rest of what Moses says and does not need to be restated in Deuteronomy 28. The enjoyment of God's presence, however, is what makes even life in the desert seem like life in Eden (cf. Ex. 33:15).

Eden apart from God's presence would be a hellish absence of the one thing that makes life sacred. Life in Eden without God would be no different from godless life in some lush place now (Breckenridge, Colorado; Beverly Hills, California; or the South of France). Heaven without God is nothing but a pretty hell.

Deuteronomy 28:1–14 opens and closes with statements that Israel will know these blessings if they obey Yahweh and do what he commands (28:1, 13–14). Between the opening and closing statements, the good things detailed in 28:3–12 are promised to the obedient.

Deuteronomy 28:3–6 presents a series of merisms. A merism is a figure of speech in which contrasting extremes are used to communicate totality. For instance, if you say, "I searched high and low," what you mean is that you searched everywhere. Similarly, to be blessed in city and field (Deut. 28:3) is to be blessed in those places and all others; to have God's blessing on the fruit of womb, ground, cattle, herds, and young of the flock is to have God's blessing on all forms of life: people, animals, and lands (28:4). To be blessed in basket and kneading bowl is to be blessed in all forms of collection and preparation (28:5), and to be blessed coming in and going out (28:5) is to be blessed everywhere you go. These verses proclaim that obedience to God results in everything you do being blessed, all forms of life around you being blessed, and your every movement from one place to another being blessed. Is it any wonder that Psalm 1 is in the Bible?

Deuteronomy 28:7 declares that God will defeat the enemies of his people, 28:8 says that everything his people store and anything they undertake will be blessed, and 28:9 announces that God will consecrate his obedient people to himself as holy. This will result in 28:10 in the nations' seeing that God's people are called by his name, with the result that the nations fear them, and 28:11 is virtually a restatement of the promise to Abraham of land, seed, and blessing (cf. Gen. 12:1–3). Deuteronomy 28:11 says God's obedient people will have abundant prosperity in the fruit of womb, livestock, and land. God will give them the rain in its season, bless the work of their hands, and cause them ever to be lending, never to be borrowing (28:12).

Could there be any way for life to be any better?

Deuteronomy 28:1–14 holds forth a vision of the good life, promising that if God's people will obey him, this life will be theirs. The life described in these blessings of the covenant holds out the possibility of pre-fall gladness in post-fall gloom. God drove Adam and Eve from the garden of Eden, but he extends to those who walk with him and obey his Word the opportunity to have an Eden-like experience though they live outside the garden's gates.

If sin results in death, how can God promise life? He can promise life because his love is stronger than death (cf. Song 8:6), and because he instituted sacrifices for atonement. In the old-covenant context, the promise of life is contingent on obedience. The obedience of Israel included their obligation to realize the guilt of their sin and offer blood sacrifice to atone for it (see, e.g., Lev. 5:1–6; 18:5). The blood sacrifices that made life possible to those who believed under the old covenant were fulfilled in Christ's death on the cross, as the author of Hebrews demonstrates.

In the Bible's grand narrative, we see that the blessings of the covenant extend the hope of God's blessing even to the work God's people do. A clear propositional truth that can be derived from the blessings of the covenant is that God's promised blessing is contingent upon obedience. Work continues to point beyond itself, with the character of God being displayed in the way God's people do their work.

God put man in the garden to work, and God intended to bless that work. What does the Bible say about how life and work changed after sin? To answer that question we look at what God said in

Genesis 3:16–17. Before we look at the judgment God spoke in Genesis 3:14–19 in response to Adam's sin in 3:1–7, however, we should note again that the blessings of the covenant pertain to (1) protection from enemies (Deut. 28:7, 10), (2) blessing on the fruit of the womb (28:4, 11), and (3) blessing on the fruit of the land (28:3, 4, 8, 11). This corresponds precisely to the words of judgment in Genesis 3:14–19, where (1) enmity is introduced between the people of God and the people of the Snake in 3:15, then (2) difficulty in childbearing is introduced in 3:16, and (3) the land is cursed in 3:17.

Judgment on God-Given Tasks (Gen. 3:16–19)

We saw what God created man and woman to accomplish in Genesis 1–2, and then we looked to Deuteronomy 28:1–14 to catch a glimpse of what life might have been like under God's blessing in the land of life, in Eden, prior to sin. We now turn to Genesis 3:16–19 to see how God's word of judgment on Adam's sin affects the work God gave humanity to do.

The woman was made to be fruitful and multiply with the man and to help him. Those two roles are made more difficult in Genesis 3:16, when God promised pain in childbearing and a desire to usurp the man's authority with corresponding harsh treatment from him. The first thing to note about the words of judgment spoken to the woman in Genesis 3:16 is that they presume the continuation of the woman's life, which is surprising in light of the prohibition and threatened penalty of death in 2:17. The ongoing life the man and woman will experience—the fact that there will be childbearing at all means the man's life, too, will continue—joins with statements made to the Snake (on which more shortly) to create hope. The words of judgment, then, are merciful. God had every right to put the man and woman to death, but he mercifully allows them to continue in life.

The life the man and woman mercifully enjoy, however, will be marked by new pain. The term rendered "pain" in both Genesis 3:16 and 3:17 occurs only three times in the Old Testament, the third being Genesis 5:29. Both the man and the woman will experience this pain in their work, and at Noah's birth, his father, Lamech, hopes that Noah will bring relief from painful toil (5:29).

Because of sin, the woman will experience a kind of pain that would not have been there had she not disobeyed God. Having been commissioned to be fruitful and multiply with the man, the woman's sin added pain to what God created her to do.

The woman was also made to help the man, but in Genesis 3:16 she is told that her "desire" will be for her husband. The term rendered "desire" occurs only three times in the Old Testament, the other two instances being Genesis 4:7 and Song of Solomon 7:10. Both shed light on the term's meaning in Genesis 3:16. In Genesis 4:7 Cain is told that sin's desire is for him, but he must "rule over it." The syntax and terminology of Genesis 3:16 and 4:7 are remarkably parallel (my very literal translation follows):

> 3:16, "and for your husband your desire, and he will rule over you."
> 4:7, "and for you its [sin's] desire, and you must rule over it."

The similarity in phrasing and vocabulary suggests that Moses intended his audience to interpret these two statements in light of each other. Sin desires Cain in Genesis 4:7 in the sense that it wants to determine his actions. Cain must rule over sin by rejecting its attempts to influence him. This would suggest that the woman's desire for her husband is a desire to determine his actions, and the man's ruling over the woman will be a rejection and suppression of her influence. The relational harmony seen in the unashamed nakedness of Genesis 2:25 is gone. No longer does the woman gladly embrace her created role of helper, and no longer does the man lovingly accept input. As a result of sin, God speaks a word of judgment over the woman that introduces relational difficulty between her and the one she was made to help.

In Genesis 3:16 God's judgment falls on the two things the woman was created to do. She will have pain in childbearing, and she will have a difficult relationship with the man she was made to help. Her sin has made her tasks harder, but in God's mercy she still has those tasks. And as we will see, hope remains.

Just as the woman's sin resulted in judgment that made it harder to accomplish what God created her to do, so also with the man. His role was to work and keep the garden, but he and the woman were driven out of the garden (3:23). He was promised, moreover, painful toil on the ground God cursed (3:17). The man is faulted for not leading the woman into holiness but following her into sin when the Lord prefaces his judgment with the words, "Because you have listened to the voice of your wife" (3:17). This reinforces what we saw above about the relationship between gender roles and work. The man failed to lead and followed instead, and in the next statement in 3:17 the Lord indicts the man for doing exactly what the Lord told him not to do. The Lord then cursed the ground in 3:17. The Serpent had been cursed in 3:14, but neither the man nor the woman was cursed. Instead, pain and complication were added to the tasks God made them to accomplish. Rather than working a blessed creation, the man will toil on a cursed ground, and he will have pain in the production of food all his life. Obstacles and impediments will frustrate the man's toil (3:18), and sweaty struggle will mark his labor until he dies (3:19).

It is interesting to observe that in the Bible's grand narrative, God's judgment falls in particular on the domains of what God made man and woman to do. From the narrative we derive propositional truths: God made man to work, but sin resulted in God's judgment. God's word of judgment against sin makes the work painful, the environment cursed, and the relationships between men and women strained. Because of sin, work will be futile, frustrating, and fatal. Everyone dies.

Work outside Eden

Is there any hope? Hope remains because work, though made difficult because of sin and judgment, continues to point beyond itself to God's character. The fact that the man and woman are allowed to continue in their work, cursed though it is, means that they still have the job of making the ways of God known in the world. But the hope for what the work points to is founded on God's word that indicates that evil will be defeated (Gen. 3:15).[16]

When we considered the curses of Genesis 3:14–19 above, we passed right over 3:14–15 to start with what God said to the woman in judgment on her tasks in 3:16. We noted, however, that what God said to the woman assumes both that she and the man will go on living and that they will have children and continue in their work.

That assumption joins with what God said to the Serpent in Genesis 3:14–15 to lay the foundation for all biblical faith and hope. God cursed the Serpent in 3:14, then told him in 3:15 that he would put enmity between the Serpent and the woman and between his seed and hers. Enmity requires that the man and the woman continue to live. Enmity between the seed of the Serpent and the seed of the woman requires that the man and the woman have offspring. God's final word in 3:15 is that the seed of the woman would bruise the

---

16. See Walter Wifall, "Gen 3:15—A Protevangelium?," *Catholic Biblical Quarterly* 36 (1974): 361–65; Jack Collins, "A Syntactical Note (Genesis 3:15): Is the Woman's Seed Singular or Plural?," *Tyndale Bulletin* 48 (1997): 139–48; and for the influence of Genesis 3:15 on the rest of the OT, James M. Hamilton Jr., "The Skull Crushing Seed of the Woman: Inner-Biblical Interpretation of Genesis 3:15," *The Southern Baptist Journal of Theology* 10, no. 2 (2006): 30–54.

head of the Serpent, while the Serpent would bruise the heel of the seed of the woman.

Believing what God said in Genesis 3:14–19, the man named his wife "Eve," mother of all living, as an act of faith (3:20). Eve's response to the births of Cain and Seth in 4:1 and 4:25 indicate that she was looking for the rise of the Serpent-crushing seed. The hope that Adam and Eve felt at the birth of their sons was built on God's word of promise that the seed of the woman would bruise the head of the Serpent. That hope brought the woman through painful childbirth, and that hope helped Adam and Eve work through the relational difficulties to forge a union that would produce offspring. That hope helped Adam in his sweaty toil and painful labor, and that hope was passed from one generation to the next.

We see the impact this promise has on expectations for work in Lamech's words at the birth of Noah in Genesis 5:29, where Lamech "called his name Noah, saying, 'Out of the ground that the LORD has cursed, this one shall bring us relief from our work and from the painful toil of our hands.'" This statement employs the concepts and terminology of Genesis 3:16–19, and, joining with 3:15, indicates that Lamech hopes that Noah will be the promised seed of the woman who will bruise the Serpent's head. Lamech further seems to hope that Noah's triumph will result in a rollback of the curses, such that relief comes from painful toil. As noted above, Noah's name employs the same root used in 2:15, when God "caused [the man] to rest in the garden of Eden" (AT).

Moses thus presents these biblical characters as understanding that the promised redeemer would bring about relief from work and painful toil. Because the language of Genesis 5:29 employs the language of 3:17, the point is not that when the seed of the woman triumphs over the Serpent, man will be relieved from work altogether, but rather that God's judgment on man's work will be removed. God made man with a task. Man was made to fill the earth, subdue it, and exercise dominion. Man was made to work.

God spoke judgment over man's work in response to man's sin.

The promise of the seed of the woman heralds a day when justice will be satisfied, curses will be removed, and work will once again be blessed by God, unimpeded and unhindered by judgment on sin.

2

Work after the Fall

Fallen, Futile, Flourishing

We have seen to this point that God made man and woman in his image for them to be fruitful and multiply, fill the earth, subdue it, and exercise dominion over the animals. Moreover, God put Adam in the garden to work and keep it, and he put the woman in the garden to help the man.

When the man and woman sinned against God, they were expelled from his presence, driven out of Eden. God put enmity between the seed of the Serpent and the seed of the woman, which means that the people who act like the Serpent and rebel against God will be at enmity with those who submit to God and obey him. God made the woman's tasks of bearing children and helping the man more difficult, and he made the man's task more difficult by cursing the ground, making toil painful and sweaty, and expelling man and woman from the garden.

We saw the indicator of hope at the birth of Noah in the ten-member genealogy that traces the descent of the seed of the woman from Adam to Noah in Genesis 5. After another ten-member genealogy tracing the seed's descent from Noah's son Shem to Abraham in Genesis 11, the promise to Abraham in 12:1–3 is layered onto the promise about the seed of the woman in 3:15.[1] In the promise of land, seed, and blessing to Abraham in 12:1–3, God promised a plot of ground where his people could once again enjoy his presence, a beachhead for the recapture of his realm. God also promised that neither the difficulty in the relationship between the man and the woman nor the pain in childbearing would keep him from blessing his people with offspring, seed, and when he promised blessing to all who bless Abraham and a curse to any who dishonor him, God promised that the seed of the woman would triumph over the seed of the Serpent. Moses presents God as declaring that anyone who opposed Abraham would be aligning with the Serpent, and for that they would be cursed like their father the Devil (cf. Gen. 3:14; 4:11; 9:25; 12:3).

All who descend from Adam live and work outside Eden, though as we have seen, in the blessings of the covenant (Leviticus 26; Deuteronomy 28) God holds out the possibility to Israel that obedience and covenant loyalty will make life edenic. In fact, we saw in Deuteronomy 28 that in the blessings of the covenant God promised land, seed, and blessing to Israel. But the best part was that God himself would be with them, as he was in Eden (Lev. 26:11–13).

As we turn our consideration to work on this side of the fall, we will see that the biblical authors present the tragic and devastating consequences of sin touching everything we are and do. We are

---

1. See T. Desmond Alexander, "Genealogies, Seed, and the Compositional Unity of Genesis," *Tyndale Bulletin* 44 (1993): 255–70; and James M. Hamilton Jr., "The Seed of the Woman and the Blessing of Abraham," *Tyndale Bulletin* 58 (2007): 253–73.

fallen, and that means our work will be fallen. Sin makes everything more difficult (cf. Gen. 4:12), and death introduces futility, meaninglessness, and a vanity into all we do. In spite of our banishment, however, the biblical authors maintain that by God's grace it is possible to flourish in the midst of fallen futility.

The scope of this project allows only for a brief cross section of what the Old Testament presents about work outside Eden, after sin. We will break our examination into three sections:

Fallen
> Identity and Work: Genesis 4
>
> A Comparison and a Killing: Genesis 4

Futile
> Vanity, Vanity, All Is Vanity: The Message of Ecclesiastes
>
> Wise Work: The Father's Teaching in Proverbs

Flourishing
> Good Examples: Joseph, Daniel, Nehemiah, Ruth
>
> How to Flourish in a Fallen World

We begin with what Moses depicts taking place in the chapter that follows man's fall into sin.

Fallen

In this section we will see that identity and work are almost inseparable and that sin makes work harder.

IDENTITY AND WORK: GENESIS 4

Adam and Eve were to subdue the earth and exercise dominion over the animals, and their firstborn son is a worker of the ground, while the second is a keeper of sheep. The description of Cain as "a worker of the ground" (4:2) uses the same verb that described Adam's job of *working* the garden in Genesis 2:15. The first family has been fruitful and multiplied, and they are pursuing the tasks God gave them.

When I have met people for the first time, I have sometimes felt a hesitation about asking them what they do for a living, as though doing so might take a reductionistic approach to who they are, as though to know what someone does is to know who they are. This hesitation probably arose from a conversation with some wiseacre who challenged me on just such a point. Look, however, at how Genesis 4:2 speaks of Cain and Abel. They are unapologetically identified by their work.

God made man to work, and from the way Moses presents the whole scene, with the man being in God's image and likeness, we know that the man was to reflect the character of God in his work. As Steve Corbett and Brian Fikkert put it, "God, who is a worker, ordained work so that humans could worship him through their work."[2] We were made to image God, and we were made to know God. God made us to reflect his character through his work. How the character of God is exercised varies with the kind of work we do.

It is of course true that there is often a good deal more to know about people than simply what they do for a living, but knowing that does tell us what they do with much of their time in much of their adult lives. Jubal in Genesis 4:21 and Tubal-cain in 4:22 are also identified by what they do, and this continues to happen across the Old Testament. So we do want to be sensitive to the reality that there is more to know about people than what they do for a living, and yet knowing what they do for a living can tell us a lot about their temperament, what kinds of things they prefer, what kinds of things

---

2. Steve Corbett and Brian Fikkert, *When Helping Hurts: How to Alleviate Poverty Without Hurting the Poor . . . and Yourself*, rev. ed. (Chicago: Moody, 2012), 109.

they may have been trained to do, and what kind of environment they inhabit while the sun shines.

Through his presentation of what happens between Cain and Abel in Genesis 4, Moses shows both how the Lord wants his people to work and how he wants them to deal with the fruit of their labor.

A COMPARISON AND A KILLING: GENESIS 4

From Genesis 4:3–7 we see that Abel honored God with the fruit of his labor, whereas Cain did not. Cain displeased the Lord, and rather than being dismayed that he failed to please God, Cain was angry (4:5). Cain should have been dismayed over the Lord's displeasure because of concern for the Lord himself. Instead he was angry, and Cain's anger at the Lord's displeasure seems to arise from Cain's concern for Cain. The Lord pressed Cain on these issues when he asked why Cain was angry (4:6) and when he assured Cain that he would be accepted if he did what was good (4:7).

Moses shows in this episode that the Lord did not receive Cain's offering because of the state of Cain's heart. Rather than working to please the Lord, and rather than using the fruit of his work to please the Lord, Cain was concerned about himself as he worked and as he decided what to do with the fruit of his work. Moses makes Cain's regard for himself, and his disregard for others, plain in what he goes on to narrate.

Moses invites his audience to compare Cain and Abel in Genesis 4:4–5. How we respond to a comparison like this shows what our hearts love. When those who love God and other people see that God does not regard what Cain has done, they will want Cain to humble himself and attempt to make things right by seeking to please the Lord. The narrative is presented such that its audience will side with the Lord rather than sympathize with Cain. Moses means for his audience to perceive that Cain loves himself, because the Lord's displeasure makes Cain feel disrespected. Rather than repent and try again, Cain murdered Abel (4:8).

Cain's murder of Abel reinforces God's purposes for humanity by showing their opposite:

- God made man in his image and likeness to represent God's character and authority in the earth, and Cain has represented the character of God's enemy (cf. John 8:44; 1 John 3:12).

- God made man to be fruitful and multiply, and Cain has set himself against God's purpose by killing rather than increasing life.

- God made man to subdue the earth and exercise dominion over the animals to help all life flourish, and instead of promoting Abel's flourishing, Cain has put an end to it.

By showing Cain rejecting God's purposes, the narrative reinforces what God's purposes are. Similarly, God's response to Cain in Genesis 4:11–12 aligns Cain with the one who has already been cursed: the Serpent in 3:14. The repetition of the words God spoke to the Serpent in 3:14 in the phrase God speaks to Cain in 4:11, "cursed you are," signals to the audience that Cain is to be identified as a seed of the Serpent. He stands with those who will be cursed: the descendants of Ham (9:25) and those who dishonor Abraham (12:3). The narrative thus teaches, "We should not be like Cain, who was of the evil one and murdered his brother" (1 John 3:12).

We also see that Cain, the "worker of the ground" (Gen. 4:2), is "cursed from the ground" (4:11), and that ground will no longer cooperate with him to give him its strength. Nor will Cain have a home or a refuge: he will be a fugitive with no place to hide, a wanderer with no real home, a farmer whose land is cursed.

This narrative shows what Proverbs 3:6 tells: man was made to know God in all his ways. In all work, we work to please God, not ourselves. Proverbs 3:9 also speaks to Cain's offering: wealth and firstfruits are to be used to honor the Lord. Moses intends to teach his audience that people do not work for themselves, nor do we reap the fruit of our work for ourselves. We live to the Lord.

When we consider what Cain's sin and judgment contribute to the broader story, we have another instance of sin resulting in God's judgment on the work one is called to do. As with Adam and Eve, God's word of judgment was directed at Cain's work. Rather than a satisfying experience of bringing God's character to bear on his tasks, Cain's work was cursed and made more difficult because of his sin. The narrative also clarifies the devastating consequences of Adam's sin. None who descend from Adam dwell naked and unashamed in the presence of God in Eden.[3] All Adam's descendants suffer his exile because of his sin, and Cain's sin exaggerated the sin of his father. God commissioned Adam and Eve to fill the world with their image-bearing offspring. Instead, by their sin, the sons of Adam filled the earth with violence (6:11). Even after the flood they used their God-given ingenuity to work for rebellion against God rather than honoring him through obedience (11:1–4).

Propositional truths that can be derived from this story include the way that all are affected by Adam's original sin (see Rom. 5:12–21) and the way that work gets harder because of God's judgment against sin. The symbolic value of the work done by Cain and Abel is worth pondering as well, along with the fruits of their labor. What

---

3. See further James M. Hamilton Jr., "Original Sin in Biblical Theology," in *Adam, the Fall, and Original Sin: Theological, Biblical, and Scientific Perspectives*, ed. Hans Madueme and Michael Reeves (Grand Rapids, MI: Baker Academic, 2014), 189–208.

the brothers did reflected their character in general, and the Lord's response to their offerings was not limited to what they brought to him but extended to what was thereby revealed about the condition of their hearts.

The Genesis 4 narrative is followed by the Genesis 5 genealogy, which has the constant refrain, "and he died." Sin brought death into the world, and the pervasiveness of death brought futility to all. Ecclesiastes teaches how to respond to that futility.

Futile

This section explores the teaching of Ecclesiastes and Proverbs on the following points: (1) sin brought death into the world, and death makes work futile (though not in an ultimate sense); (2) fathers are to teach their sons to be diligent and faithful; and (3) women are called to work in the context of family. I place the teaching from Proverbs under the heading "futile" because like the teaching of Ecclesiastes this instruction applies in spite of the frustrations of the fallen world. In both Proverbs and Ecclesiastes we have instruction on how to make the best of a broken world.

VANITY, VANITY, ALL IS VANITY: THE MESSAGE OF ECCLESIASTES

I hated all my toil in which I toil under the sun, seeing that I must leave it to the man who will come after me, and who knows whether he will be wise or a fool? Yet he will be master of all for which I toiled and used my wisdom under the sun. This also is vanity. So I turned about and gave my heart up to despair over all the toil of my labors under the sun, because sometimes a person who has toiled with wisdom and knowledge and skill must leave everything to be enjoyed by someone who did not toil for it. This also is vanity and a great evil. What has a man from all the toil and striving of heart with which he toils beneath the sun? For all his days are full of sorrow, and his work is a vexation. Even in the night his heart does not rest. This also is vanity. There is nothing better for a person than that he should eat and drink and find enjoyment in his toil. This also, I saw, is from the hand of God, for apart from him who can eat or who can have enjoyment? (Eccles. 2:18–25)

The toilsome, laborious nature of the futility of life and work is a major theme in the book of Ecclesiastes. The book is unflinching in its treatment of death's long shadow but just as resolute in maintaining that there is a good way to respond. This word *good* is in fact key to the book's message.

Ecclesiastes wrestles with the realities that flow from God's word of judgment on man's work in Genesis 3:17–19. Work will be painful and frustrating and then comes death. And yet there is hope, and Ecclesiastes links up with Old Testament hope through the reference to the "son of David" in 1:1 and then the reference to the Shepherd in 12:11. Framed with those links to the hope for the future king from David's line, the Redeemer who will shepherd God's people, Ecclesiastes presents the pain of life outside Eden with complete honesty.

Having announced the vanity of all things (Eccles. 1:2), Qohelet ("the Preacher") asks, "What does man gain by all the toil at which he toils under the sun?" (1:3). The author tells of how he explored pleasure (2:1–11), and his conclusion is a reflection on how his labor was vanity and grasping for the wind (2:10–11). He relates how he explored wisdom (2:12–17), and his conclusion is that the work done under the sun is vanity and grasping for the wind (2:17).

He then explores various problems with the laborious toil in which humanity is engaged: the results of our toil will be left to another (2:18–26); there is a right time for everything, but often that right time eludes us (3:1–4:6); God said it is not good for man to be alone, but often we find ourselves tasked with work that must be done in solitude (4:7–16); and then there is the problem of enjoying what we have gained by our toil (5:1–6:9).[4]

Every one of these sections ends with Solomon's advice on how to respond to the futility and vanity of the work we must do under the sun. Qohelet starts out asking what is *good* for the sons of men to do in their short lives (2:3), and he repeatedly answers that there is nothing more *good* (i.e., better) for man to do than to eat, drink, and enjoy his work, because the ability to do this is a gift of God.

Seven times Solomon reinforces this message. In this listing of the passages that follows, I have italicized the references to (1) what is good (nothing better), (2) eating and drinking in enjoyment of God's goodness, (3) the enjoyment of one's work, and (4) the ability to do so being a gift of God (or man's lot, cf. Prov. 16:33).

- There is *nothing better* for a person than that he should *eat and drink* and *find enjoyment in his toil*. This also, I saw, is *from the hand of God*, for apart from him who can eat or who can have enjoyment? (Eccles. 2:24–25)

- I perceived that there is *nothing better* for them than to be joyful and to do good as long as they live; also that everyone should *eat and drink* and *take pleasure in all his toil*—this is *God's gift* to man. (Eccles. 3:12–13)

---

4. I am following the structure of the book set forth convincingly in Addison G. Wright, "The Riddle of the Sphinx: The Structure of the Book of Qoheleth," *Catholic Biblical Quarterly* 30 (1968): 313–34; Addison G. Wright, "The Riddle of the Sphinx Revisited: Numerical Patterns in the Book of Qoheleth," *Catholic Biblical Quarterly* 42 (1980): 38–51; and Addison G. Wright, "Additional Numerical Patterns in Qoheleth," *Catholic Biblical Quarterly* 45 (1983): 32–43.

- So I saw that there is *nothing better* than that a man should *rejoice in his work*, for that is *his lot*. Who can bring him to see what will be after him? (Eccles. 3:22)

- Behold, what I have seen to be *good* and fitting is to *eat and drink* and *find enjoyment in all the toil* with which one toils under the sun the few days of his life that *God has given him*, for this is *his lot*. Everyone also to whom *God has given* wealth and possessions *and power to enjoy them*, and *to accept his lot* and rejoice in his toil—*this is the gift of God*. (Eccles. 5:18–19; cf. 6:1–2)

- And I commend joy, for man has *nothing better* under the sun but to *eat and drink* and be *joyful*, for this will go with him *in his toil* through the days of his life that *God has given him* under the sun. (Eccles. 8:15)

- Go, *eat* your bread with joy, and *drink* your wine with a merry heart, for God has already approved what you do. Let your garments be always white. Let not oil be lacking on your head. *Enjoy life* with the wife whom you love, all the days of your vain life that he has given you under the sun, because *that is your portion in life and in your toil at which you toil* under the sun. Whatever your hand finds to do, do it with your might, for there is no work or thought or knowledge or wisdom in Sheol, to which you are going. (Eccles. 9:7–10)

- So if a person lives many years, *let him rejoice* in them all; but let him remember that the days of darkness will be many. All that comes is vanity. *Rejoice*, O young man, in your youth, and *let your heart cheer you* in the days of your youth. Walk in the ways of your heart and the sight

of your eyes. But know that for all these things God will
bring you into judgment. Remove vexation from your
heart, and put away pain from your body, for youth and
the dawn of life are vanity. (Eccles. 11:8–10)

In the very good creation before man sinned, God gave man good
food (Gen. 1:29–31), work (Gen. 1:28; 2:15), and the companionship
of a wife (Gen. 2:18–25). Sin brought death into the world, but the
preacher in Ecclesiastes nevertheless teaches his audience to enjoy
God's good gifts of food, work, and companionship; similar notes
were sounded in Psalm 128. The ability to do so is a merciful gift
from God, as Ecclesiastes 6:1–2 makes clear:

There is an evil that I have seen under the sun, and it lies
heavy on mankind: a man to whom God gives wealth, possessions, and honor, so that he lacks nothing of all that he
desires, yet God does not give him power to enjoy them, but
a stranger enjoys them. This is vanity; it is a grievous evil.

The book of Ecclesiastes deals not with a major turning point
in the outworking of the Bible's salvation-historical drama but with
the ordinary humdrum of everyday life. This book looks the futility
of life in a fallen world full in the face, recognizing that death, the
bane of every man, renders all work temporary. Old age makes every
pleasure a passing cloud (see esp. Eccles. 11:7–12:8). We do not know
what will become of our efforts once we are gone (9:1–11:6). And
yet in God's mercy life can be enjoyed, food and drink can refresh,
and joy can be found in labor. In all this we should fear God, walk
in the ways of the Torah, and know that judgment is coming (11:9;
12:13–14).

So there is nothing better than for man to eat and drink and
enjoy his work, and if one can do this, it is God's gift to him, even in

the making of many books and the study so wearisome to the flesh (12:12).

The book of Proverbs is even more specific and detailed on how to flourish in the midst of fallen futility.

WISE WORK: THE FATHER'S TEACHING IN PROVERBS

Imagine two houses. One house is built by Lady Wisdom (Prov. 9:1, 4), and the other house is held by Madame Folly (9:14; cf. 7:16–17). Those who enter Lady Wisdom's home find life (9:6, 11). Those who go to Madame Folly die (9:18; cf. 7:22–27).

Those who learn from Lady Wisdom know that her teaching is better than money (2:4; 3:13–16; 8:11, 18–19), but they also learn diligence and prudence from her, which lead to lasting wealth (10:4). By contrast, those who indulge Lady Folly become impoverished sluggards (6:6, 10–11) and pursue wealth in illegal ways (1:10–19), and the treasure they acquire does not profit (10:2).

The different ways of living represented by these two ladies also result in different sleep patterns. The wise lie down to sleep in security, and their rest is sweet and refreshing (3:24), with the Bible's teaching protecting them as they rest and the Bible's words rolling around in their noggins as they wake up in the morning (6:22). The consorts of Lady Folly, by contrast, cannot rest because their evil desires prod them to more and more late-night searching for the ever-elusive satisfaction they seek (4:16), and then they overindulge in sleep (6:9). Their slack hands only increase their poverty (10:4). The wise are the kind who harvest when the grain is ripe, while the foolish are sleeping when they should be working. And then it's too late (10:5).

Like Ecclesiastes, the book of Proverbs is not advancing the salvation-historical narrative but giving instruction on how to live as the years roll by. Also like Ecclesiastes and Psalm 128, the book's instruction commends a picture of the good life characterized by diligent, faithful, and wise work done by a man who is providing for and protecting his wife and children, teaching his sons to do to the same. That is to say, as with Psalm 128, Ecclesiastes, and Genesis 1–2, Proverbs commends a husbanding kind of work: labor done to benefit others, the fruits of which are enjoyed in the context of one's family; and a sense of symbiotic balance arises from the teaching of the whole book.

Fathers were commanded in Deuteronomy 6:7 to teach their sons the Torah, and kings were instructed in Deuteronomy 17:14–20 to know and walk by Torah. In the tribal patriarchy of Old Testament Israel, the king was in a sense the father of the nation (cf. 1 Sam. 24:11, 16). King Solomon, son of David, heir to the 2 Samuel 7 promises, is an obedient and fatherly king instructing his sons in the Torah through the book of Proverbs.

In Proverbs the father teaches his son that robbers and pirates ambush their own lives (1:8–19, esp. 1:18). Lady Wisdom makes herself known in the markets at the beginning of the book (1:20–33), and the noble wife is active in the markets at the end (31:14–15). Solomon teaches that the one who treasures wisdom and seeks it like silver and hidden treasure will find that wisdom does for him what people want money to do for them—and more (2:1–22; 3:14–16). The goal of life is not to be rich but to walk with God and honor him with wealth (3:6, 9–10).

Poverty will be avoided by ant-like diligence and preparation for winter at harvest time (6:6–11). Calamity will be avoided by honest, straightforward, nondeceptive dealings with others (6:12–15).

WOMEN AND WORK: PROVERBS 31

Just as we have seen much to this point that places a man's work in the context of his family, the statements about the working woman in Proverbs 31:10–31 place her activity in the context of family. Her husband's heart trusts in her, and he has no lack of gain because of her (31:11), she does him good all her days (31:12), she provides food for her household (31:15, 21, 27), her husband's standing in the city is increased by her virtue (31:23), and her children and husband rise up to bless and praise her (31:28). The assumption clearly is that once a girl reaches the age to be married, she will do so, and the text celebrates wives who so live that they bless all who know them. Her work is done willingly (31:13), she is diligent to rise early to do it and refuses to be idle (31:15, 27), she thoughtfully considers fields she might purchase for fruitful cultivation (31:16), she sells merchandise she worked hard to produce at a profit (31:18–19, 24), she is generous to the poor with that profit (31:20), and she works to provide all-weather gear and comfortable bedding (31:21–22). Much more could be said about this passage, but for our purposes we can observe an overt expectation that women will become wives and mothers who will labor to provide for the needs of their families while also blessing the wider community. We also see no conflict in this chapter between a woman being a virtuous wife and noble mother while engaging in real estate speculation and cultivation and also manufacturing clothing for her own family's use and the wider market. With the chapter opening and closing with statements of what a blessing this woman is to her husband (31:10–12, 28–31), her work is framed as though she is helping him to work and keep his garden.

Proverbs 31 does not speak of unmarried women, though it inculcates the expectation that single ladies will aspire to be the kind of wife described here. The book of Ruth (see below) describes the situation of a single lady, and Paul gives instructions for widows old and young in 1 Timothy 5:9–16. For those who might never marry, the Old Testament covenant community provided a family structure that finds its new covenant analog in the church, the family of God.

In some ways the book of Proverbs amounts to a pithy restatement of the blessings and curses of the covenant. Those who walk with God, fear him, and follow his instructions will live, while those who disregard God and his Word face his personal displeasure. Interestingly, the book is set in the context of family: the father calls his son to wisdom throughout, depicting wisdom as a noble, virtuous, life-giving wife. In this context, to work is to fulfill the task for which man was made. Work done with wisdom symbolizes the realization of God's purpose to have his image reflected by those made in his likeness, for God himself did his work with the aid of wisdom (Prov. 8:22–31).

Flourishing

We turn our attention from Wisdom Literature to exemplary figures in biblical narratives who walked in wisdom. To pursue biblical theology as the interpretive perspective of the biblical authors when considering narrative literature includes asking what those authors meant to promote and what they meant to discourage. Understanding an author's perspective means being able to determine from the story the author tells how the author meant for his audience to respond.

Often the biblical authors present stories of people whose lives of faith they want their audience to emulate. As human beings we need to be shown "the people of old [who] received their commendation" (Heb. 11:2), to have "so great a cloud of witnesses" (Heb. 12:1) testify to us of how we ought to walk in faith, and to understand the examples that "were written down for our instruction" (1 Cor. 10:11), that we might be transformed into the image of the one who left us "an example, so that [we] might follow in his steps" (1 Pet. 2:21).

We can hardly imagine how to begin to live unless we have examples, people who have blazed the trail before us. Consider, then, three men and one woman who flourished in the midst of fallen futility.

Good Examples: Joseph, Daniel, Nehemiah, and Ruth

The examples of Joseph, Daniel, Nehemiah, and Ruth are relevant for a biblical theology of work for a number of reasons. Foremost among these are the ways that these men serve as types of Christ and this woman became a messianic matriarch. The men were faithful while living under foreign powers, facing opposition and persecution, and through them the Lord brought deliverance for his people. Ruth, meanwhile, was a Gentile who married a kinsman redeemer in what came to be the Davidic line. Joseph and Daniel were both put in a pit. Joseph's brothers assumed he was long dead, and everyone thought the lions would eat Daniel. Both men were unexpectedly found alive and brought deliverance or revelations of it. The lives of both anticipated the pattern of the one who would be rejected, crucified, dead, and buried, only to rise in triumph, securing salvation.[5] Jesus fulfilled the typological patterns seen in the lives of these men, and we are called to follow in the footsteps of Jesus, being transformed into his image. Joseph, Daniel, and Nehemiah, then, teach us Christlikeness, and Ruth's story shows God's remarkable providence in the Messiah's . line of descent.

In addition to being types of Christ, these men lived and worked in salvation-historical settings analogous to the one we find ourselves in today. They lived prior to Christ, but in their day there was no kingdom of God. Joseph lived prior to the establishment of Israel as a nation, Daniel and Nehemiah after the nation was destroyed. They had no earthly kingdom but lived under the powers of the world. They worked for those who did not seek God's kingdom but their

5. See Mitchell L. Chase, "Resurrection Hope in Daniel 12:2: An Exercise in Biblical Theology," PhD dissertation, The Southern Baptist Theological Seminary, 2013; Samuel Cyrus Emadi, "Covenant, Typology, and the Story of Joseph: A Literary-Canonical Examination of Genesis 37–50," PhD dissertation, The Southern Baptist Theological Seminary, 2016; and James M. Hamilton Jr., "Was Joseph a Type of the Messiah? Tracing the Typological Identification between Joseph, David, and Jesus," *The Southern Baptist Journal of Theology* 12 (2008): 52–77.

own, and they found ways to be faithful in spite of the surrounding worldliness. Through their stories the biblical authors teach us what it means to seek first God's kingdom, even while working in the government of a kingdom of this world. Ruth's story is similar though different at points. Her days were those of the judges, when there was no king in Israel and everyone did what was right in his own eyes. In spite of the decadent circumstances, she too found a way to be faithful. We consider them each in turn.

Joseph. Pursuing biblical theology as an attempt to understand and embrace the interpretive perspective of the biblical authors with respect to Joseph entails understanding the part Joseph plays in the story of Genesis, and more broadly in the Pentateuch. Doing a pencil-sketch outline of Genesis on this point would look something like this: the very good creation in Genesis 1–2 is spoiled by sin in Genesis 3. God makes promises in Genesis 3, however, that point to the restoration of all things and the triumph over evil. The promises are passed down through the generations in the genealogies to Abraham, to whom the Lord elaborates on the original promise in the blessing of Genesis 12:1–3. The promise to Abraham is passed to Isaac, then to Jacob, and at the end of the book of Genesis we find a seed of the woman in whom all the families of the earth are being blessed.

Moving beyond Genesis, in the broad narrative of the Pentateuch, Joseph prepares the way for the rest of his family's descent into Egypt, and the Joseph narrative at the end of Genesis immediately precedes the exodus narrative at the beginning of the book of Exodus. As later biblical authors pointed to a new exodus, there are indications that they expected a new Joseph as well.[6]

Consider Joseph's story against the backdrop of the promises of

---

6. See the evidence for this in James M. Hamilton Jr., *With the Clouds of Heaven: The Book of Daniel in Biblical Theology*, New Studies in Biblical Theology (Downers Grove, IL: IVP Academic, 2014), 221–35.

land, seed, and blessing made to Abraham in Genesis 12:1–3. Moses presents the passing down of the promises to Isaac, then to Jacob, and as a result his audience can assume that Jacob's family would have known about the blessings promised to Abraham. Joseph and his brothers would have desired the fulfillment of those promises: to have land, offspring, and God's blessing on their lives.

If Joseph's desire was to possess the land of promise, his reality was being sold as a slave and taken to Egypt. If Joseph's desire was to perpetuate the line of the seed of the woman through his offspring, his reality was to be married to the daughter of an Egyptian priest. If Joseph sought God's blessing, by the world's standard of measure it would seem that he was cursed. And yet we never read of any sins Joseph committed, and we repeatedly read that the Lord was with him.

As a result of God's being with Joseph, Joseph prospered as a slave, then in prison, and then was unexpectedly exalted over all Egypt. By the end of his life, though still outside the land, he gave instructions for his bones to be buried in the Land of Promise (Gen. 50:24–26; Heb. 11:22).[7] Joseph married an Egyptian, through whom God gave him seed. Not only did he have offspring; they received the blessing from Jacob (Gen. 48:15–16; cf. 1 Chron. 5:1–2). It may have seemed to the eyes of the world that Joseph was cursed and afflicted, but all the world was blessed through him as the Lord used him to provide food for all the families of the earth in the devastating famine (cf. Gen. 47:25 with Gen. 12:1–3).

Joseph experienced anticipatory fulfillments of the blessing of Abraham. His regard for God kept him from sin with Potiphar's wife (Gen. 39:9). The Lord's favor gave him good standing with those over him (39:3–4, 21). With God's help, Joseph proposed a plan for preparing for famine that provided food for Egypt and all

---

7. Joseph believed that God's promise transcended his own death, and Joseph believed that God would raise him from the dead and grant him the joy of fulfilled hopes in the land of life.

the earth (41:28–36). Joseph's dealings with his brothers show him to be shrewd as a serpent and gentle as a dove: he forgave them and provided for them.

In the midst of his work for Pharaoh in Egypt, Joseph probably did not know God's Psalm 105:17 plan for his life: "He had sent a man ahead of them, Joseph, who was sold as a slave." If Joseph did not know that he was sent ahead of Israel into Egypt, preparing the way for the exodus (cf. Ps. 105:16–38), Moses did. Moses arranged his material such that the Joseph story is followed by the exodus story.

The narrative of Joseph's life is a narrative of faithful work while suffering for doing good and experiencing inaugurations of God's blessing in the midst of affliction. The pattern of Joseph's life is a pattern fulfilled in Jesus, a pattern that informs the identity and expectations of those who follow Jesus.

Moses presents a Joseph who does not know everything that God is doing but who nevertheless fears God, flees temptation, loves God and neighbor in his work, forgives those who wronged him, and experiences God's presence in the midst of his difficulties. His children receive the blessing, pointing again to the balance of work and family. Joseph lived outside of God's land, before the giving of God's law, but he nevertheless experienced God's presence and favor. The admonitions of Proverbs instruct readers of the Bible on the particulars of living and working in ways that enable people to enjoy God's presence and blessing as Joseph did.

Daniel. For the purposes of this study, what is noteworthy about the book of Daniel is the relationship between the narratives of what Daniel and his friends experienced in Daniel 1–6 and the apocalyptic predictions of Daniel 7–12. The connection between the two halves of the book can be briefly stated as follows: the kind of faithfulness in the face of oppression and persecution that Daniel 7–12 calls for is the kind of faithfulness in the face of oppression and persecution illustrated in Daniel 1–6. It is as though the history of the seed of the Serpent's opposition to the seed of the woman in Daniel 1–6 is projected onto the future in Daniel 7–12, and the wise of the future are called to respond as Daniel and his friends did in the past.

Nebuchadnezzar attacked the temple (Dan. 1:2), as will the future kings in the visions of Daniel 8, 9, and 11 (8:11–13; 9:26–27; 11:31). God gave Daniel and his friends wisdom (1:17), and through the message of Daniel he gives wisdom to those who will face the future trials the book predicts (11:33, 35; 12:3).

Daniel and his friends model faithfulness to the Lord in spite of their situation: they sought to abide by the Mosaic food regulations though in captivity (Dan. 1:8–20); they trusted God and prayed for revelation when they were put in an impossible and life-threatening situation (2:13–23); Daniel's friends refused to commit idolatry though threatened with execution (3:8–18); Daniel spoke unwelcome truths to the kings Nebuchadnezzar and Belshazzar and called them to repentance (4:19–27; 5:17–28); and Daniel refused to stop praying to the Lord though threatened with execution (6:10–15).

Like Joseph before them, Daniel and his friends model faithfulness in work as high-ranking officials involved in the administration of a foreign kingdom. From all of these men we see a willingness to speak the truth in love. Joseph corrected mistaken assumptions about where the ability to interpret the dream originated, giving glory to God (Gen. 41:16). Daniel did the same (Dan. 2:27–28). Joseph suggested a wise course of action (Gen. 41:33–36), as did Daniel (Dan. 4:27).

With Daniel and his friends we see several different responses to conflicts over the free exercise of religion and conscience. When their freedom to eat according to the dictates of conscience is threatened in Daniel 1, Daniel and his friends engage in a judicious appeal and propose a test to determine whether what they propose is beneficial.

God blesses their efforts, and the young men remain faithful. When the worshipers of the true God are threatened in Daniel 2 with a death sentence against all in their professional class, they request time and commit themselves to prayer for mercy, and again God blesses them by revealing the king's dream to Daniel.

Daniel and his friends seek to defuse tension between themselves and the idolaters in power in chapters 1 and 2, and that pattern appears to continue in chapter 3. A demand is made that all bow to an idolatrous statue. Daniel is never mentioned in the chapter, suggesting that he managed to stay off the radar in that conflict. His friends apparently tried to do the same, but they were outed by malicious adversaries (3:8). When the conflict became unavoidable, Shadrach, Meshach, and Abednego refused to bow (3:16–18). The fact that God delivered them from the fiery furnace encourages the audience of the book of Daniel to follow in the footsteps of their faithfulness.

Daniel's response to the king's dream in Daniel 4:19 reveals genuine affection for the king and authentic concern for his welfare. Daniel's obvious concern enveloped his call for the king to "break off [his] sins by practicing righteousness, and [his] iniquities by showing mercy to the oppressed" (4:27). Daniel's response to Belshazzar reveals a freedom from the enticement of worldly luxury that ensures the verity and purity of Daniel's ministry (5:17).

As his friends avoided open confrontation in Daniel 3, Daniel did not provoke his opponents in Daniel 6, though neither did he allow them to intimidate him into altering his disciplined worship of the Lord in prayer (6:1–13). Daniel knew that his life was at stake, and he continued to pray to Yahweh. Once again, the Lord delivered Daniel by closing the mouths of the lions.

The book of Daniel teaches that the people of God should walk in accordance with the Torah (Daniel 1), pray to the Lord in crisis (Daniel 2), refuse to bow to idols for deliverance (Daniel 3), love pagans and tell them the truth (Daniel 4), remain free from worldly temptations to corruption (Daniel 5), and never allow pagan threats to keep them from praying and worshiping the Lord (Daniel 6).

This narrative teaching in Daniel 1–6 prepares Daniel's audience to respond to the future king who will "wear out the saints of the Most High," which saints "shall be given into his hand" in Daniel 7:25. It prepares them to face the future king under whom they will be "trampled underfoot" in 8:10 and 8:13. Readers are trained by the book to withstand the one who will "put an end to sacrifice and offering" in 9:27 and equipped to resist the one who will "seduce with flattery those who violate the covenant" in 11:32. The book of Daniel instructs people who will live and work as those "who know their God" and thereby be able to "stand firm and take action" (11:32).

The book of Daniel teaches that even if the Lord does not deliver everyone the way he delivered Daniel and his friends, we should nevertheless be faithful to the Lord (cf. 3:17–18), who will raise the dead and reward the righteous (12:2–3).

Nehemiah. Much could be said about Nehemiah as a type of Christ,[8] about the way he must have been a man of Bible study and prayer for the book bearing his name to read as it does, and about the similarities between Joseph, Daniel, and Nehemiah as Jews serving in foreign courts. For our purposes here, however, I want to highlight what the book of Nehemiah shows us about Nehemiah as a worker.

Between hearing the report of the state of things in Jerusalem in November–December of 446 BC (Neh. 1:1) and having the opportunity to make requests of the king in March–April of 445 BC (2:1–4), Nehemiah was evidently praying and fasting (1:4–11). From the specificity of the requests he makes, however, we can see that he was also planning and calculating. Nehemiah knows exactly what

---

8. See the chapter on "Messianic Hope in Ezra–Nehemiah" in James M. Hamilton Jr., *Exalting Christ in Ezra and Nehemiah*, Christ-Centered Exposition (Nashville: Broadman, 2014), 227–41.

he wants (2:5); he knows how long the journey and the project will take (2:6), what kinds of passports he needs (2:7), and where to get the building materials (2:8). Nehemiah has studied the ants (cf. Prov. 6:6–8) and learned wisdom for work.

Through his constant prayer and recognition of God's hand (e.g., Neh. 1:4–11; 2:4; 2:8, 18), we see that Nehemiah worked in reliance on God's power and guidance (cf. 2:12). From his willingness to take up arms we see his commitment to the work (4:13–20). From his long hours and not changing clothes we see an example of vigilant and constant work (4:21–23). From the way he stood down oppressors we see a commitment to justice and righteousness at work (5:1–13). From his refusal to be distracted we see his devotion to his work (6:3). And from the completion of the project we see the fruit of Nehemiah's work (6:15–16).

Having rebuilt the wall, Nehemiah set about rebuilding the people, a project more challenging and frustrating than the work on the wall (Nehemiah 7–13). From his prayers for God to remember him, we see Nehemiah's recognition that his work would be weighed at a future assize, that there would be rewards and punishments, and we see Nehemiah praying for the Lord to be merciful and gracious to him on that day.

Ruth. Most English translations place the book of Ruth between Judges and 1 Samuel, which is appropriate given the way that the book of Ruth ends with the genealogy of David. Editions of the Old Testament in Hebrew, however, tend to place Ruth after Proverbs, which is also appropriate as Ruth is an example of the kind of woman described in Proverbs 31.

Ruth was a Moabitess who had apparently been married for a decade but had no children (Ruth 1:4–5). Deuteronomy 23:3 says that no Moabite may enter the assembly of the Lord, but Ruth repudiated her kinsmen and their gods when she insisted to Naomi not only that the people of Israel would be her people but also that the God of Israel would be her God (Ruth 1:16). Having found a place among God's people, Ruth sought to provide for Naomi in a way that was in keeping with the Mosaic Law, which made provision for widows to glean in the fields (Ruth 2:2; cf. Deut. 24:19). Ruth earned a good reputation as a hard worker (Ruth 2:6–7), and everyone in the community could see that she was providing for Naomi in a way that was self-sacrificial and loving (2:11).

Ruth's faith and godliness are displayed when Naomi comes up with a scheme to force Boaz to do his duty as a kinsman redeemer (3:1–4). Naomi's comments are very suggestive. She wants Ruth to perfume herself and go to the threshing floor, where only the men would be, and once Boaz has finished eating and drinking, Naomi tells Ruth to "uncover his feet"—language at once suggestive and euphemistic—and do what Boaz tells her to do (3:3–4).

This places Ruth in a delicate predicament. On the one hand, she has standing in the community by virtue of her relationship with Naomi. On the other hand, Naomi is suggesting that she take actions that would place her in a most compromised and vulnerable position. Given what she does, we can say that when Ruth answers in 3:5, "All that you say I will do," what she means is that she will do everything Naomi has said and *nothing* that Naomi has so suggestively hinted at.

Naomi clearly intended for things to happen when Ruth uncovered the feet of Boaz and lay down there. Ruth, however, approached Boaz so stealthily that when he was startled awake in the middle of the night he was surprised to find her there (3:7–8). From what she says to him, we see that she has considered how to speak to Boaz so as to provoke him to godliness. Boaz had earlier blessed Ruth in the name of "the Lord, the God of Israel, under whose wings you have come to take refuge" (2:12). Ruth seems to remind him of this in the middle of the night at the threshing floor when she says, "Spread your wings over your servant, for you are a redeemer" (3:9). It is as though she is asking Boaz to be the means by which the Lord shelters her with his wings.

Boaz then takes steps to protect Ruth's reputation and do everything lawfully, culminating in his marriage to Ruth. Then though she was married for ten years with apparently no children, the Lord blesses her with a child who becomes the grandfather of King David (4:13, 21–22).

Much more could be said about this dramatic and exhilarating story, but here we are concerned with what it says about a single female, a widow, at work. The following observations can be made. First, she sought work authorized by the law of Moses. Second, she worked hard in the service not only of herself but also to benefit Naomi, who was dependent upon her. Third, she worked in such a way that she gained a good reputation among her fellow workers and also in the community at large. Fourth and finally, she worked in a way that was sexually pure, preserving chastity even as she honored Naomi who had wickedly suggested that she seduce Boaz.

God richly blessed Ruth's faithfulness.

How to Flourish in a Fallen World

The post–Genesis 3 and pre–Matthew 1 world is the setting for all that we have seen in this chapter. Adam's descendants have been plunged into sin and exiled from Eden, but God gave good instruction for his people. In the teaching of Ecclesiastes and Proverbs, the people of God are taught many things about how to live and work in the fallen world. That teaching on how to work is complemented by the positive example of those who worked well that we have surveyed in our brief consideration of Joseph, Daniel, Nehemiah, and Ruth.

If we were to summarize the instructions and the examples, we might say something like this: know God in all your ways (Prov. 3:5). Enjoy your work and its fruits as God's gift to you (cf. the seven statements to this effect in Ecclesiastes). Hope in the promises and bless the world (Gen. 12:1–3). Live and work the way that Joseph, Daniel, and Nehemiah did: seeking to hallow God's name and to see his kingdom come and his will be done—in reliance on him for daily bread, forgiveness of sin, and deliverance from evil—for his is the kingdom, the power, and the glory forever.

Work under the Old Covenant

We have not looked at everything the Old Testament has to say on the topic of work post-fall and pre-Christ, but from what we have encountered we can accurately summarize the biblical authors' perspective on work in the old-covenant era. In terms of the wider narrative, we have seen that man's responsibility to work and to image forth God's character in work was not abrogated by his sin and expulsion from the garden. God's instructions and presence with his people provide the gracious help necessary for man's tasks, and those who embrace biblical wisdom will themselves understand and help others to do the same (Dan. 11:33; 12:10).

The Bible's instructions for work enable those who believe to experience God's presence and blessing though exiled from Eden. God's judgment on sin in Genesis 3:14–19 touches every area of life, and in the lives of Joseph, Daniel, and Nehemiah we see how the enmity between the seed of the Serpent and the seed of the woman extends even to the work the righteous seek to do. In the book of Ruth we see how a Gentile widow saw the stakes of the conflict between the seed of the woman and the seed of the Serpent, chose to identify with God and his people, and was mercifully incorporated into the line of descent of the seed of the woman. And God blessed her work. Joseph's brothers ended his career as a shepherd. Daniel's enemies sought to thwart him and keep him from working and even living. And Nehemiah's enemies tried to distract him, intimidate him, ambush him, and sabotage him as he worked. By working with integrity in obedience to God's commands, by relying on the Lord and crying out to him in prayer, and by believing God's promises, these men and this woman fixed their hearts on the city that has foundations (cf. Heb. 11:10, 16) and sought the welfare of the city in which God had placed them (cf. Jer. 29:7).

Their work pointed beyond itself as they sought to exemplify God's character in what they did. By imaging forth God's likeness, they typified the one who was to come—and in Ruth's case joined his line of descent, the one who would build God's temple and rule God's kingdom. These anticipatory types of Christ—Joseph, Daniel, and Nehemiah—along with Ruth the matriarchal woman of valor, were imitators of God in their work, and they are examples for us, for whose instruction their stories were written (cf. Rom. 15:4).

3

Redemption

Work Now That Christ Has Risen

In chapter 1 we looked at what Genesis 1–2 shows us about God's intentions for man in the very good creation prior to sin, with some help from the blessings of the covenant in Deuteronomy 28. In chapter 2 we considered the way that God continued to pursue his creational purposes by making promises to Abraham and his seed, then covenanting with that seed at Sinai. To see what the biblical authors understood as God's intentions for everyday life and work under the old covenant, we considered the positive strategy for dealing with fallen futility in the exhortation to flourish in Ecclesiastes, along with the wisdom for developing this kind of skill at living in Proverbs.

We have seen that God created man to work, that sin has made fallen work futile, but that God's merciful instructions nevertheless enable flourishing. We now consider how what Jesus accomplished on the cross redeems and frees people to work for God's glory.

It is perhaps worth reflecting at this point that at one level we are progressing along the salvation-historical storyline in that we have moved from creation, to the old covenant, and now turn our attention to the new covenant. At another level, however, in our consideration of the topic of work we have gone off-line—off the salvation-historical storyline, anyway—in that we are not examining *events* in sequence. We considered old-covenant Wisdom Literature in chapter 2, and here in chapter 3 our attention is focused mainly on Pauline *instruction*, with a word from his friend James. Just as the old-covenant Wisdom Literature cannot be understood apart from the covenant, Paul's new-covenant wisdom cannot be understood apart from the new-covenant realities inaugurated by the death, resurrection, and ascension of the Lord Jesus.

The Mosaic law was not given until after the exodus from Egypt, and in the same way, Paul's instructions come after the death and resurrection of Jesus. God first redeems his people, then he instructs them on how they are to live. Paul addresses people formerly enslaved to sin who have had their chains broken and their debts paid, and he shines the light of God's instructions, mercifully, graciously teaching them how to live their new lives. The body of this chapter will be given to the instructions, but to keep these from seeming in any way legalistic, the instructions must be seen where Paul puts them, against a wider backdrop of Christ's work and victory on the cross as the Lamb who was slain for the sins of his people.

Seeking a biblical theology of work, we are probing the Bible to find how the biblical authors themselves viewed this topic. We have been looking at the place of work in the Bible's big story, the propositions about work that can be derived from it, and work's symbolic value. As we turn to work in the new covenant, we find that in his letters Paul will summarize relevant aspects of the story for his audience, then give his readers the propositional truths that can be derived from the story in the form of commands. The body of this chapter seeks to synthesize those commands, but these belong in the context of the wider story.

In that wider story, the long-promised Messiah, the one who would bruise the Serpent's head in Genesis 3:15, came at the right time (Mark 1:15; Rom. 5:6; Gal. 4:4). God definitively authenticated him through the signs and wonders he did (Acts 2:22). Fulfilling the typological pattern of the righteous sufferer seen in the likes of Joseph, Moses, David, Elijah, and others, Jesus was rejected and crucified (cf. Acts 7). Bringing the Passover to fulfillment, by the blood of Jesus God redeemed his people (1 Cor. 5:7; Rev. 1:5).

Jesus came as the king from David's line (Rom. 1:3), as the individual representative of Israel, the true vine (John 15:1). When he was killed, the one who stood for the nation was struck down by God's wrath, fulfilling what was typified by Israel's exile from the land (John 2:19). When he rose from the dead, Jesus set in motion the new exodus and return from exile—in fulfillment of Ezekiel 37 and Hosea 6:2, where return from exile is symbolically presented as resurrection from the dead (cf. 1 Cor. 15:3–4).

Jesus then ascended into heaven and poured out the promised eschatological blessing of the Holy Spirit (Isa. 32:15; Joel 2:28–32; Acts 2:33). The Spirit indwells the church as the new temple (1 Cor. 3:16; 6:19).[1]

The New Testament presents Jesus as the fulfillment of the Passover (e.g., 1 Cor. 5:7), and the church consists of those bought from slavery to sin at the price of his blood (Rom. 6:17–18; 1 Cor. 6:20).

---

[1]. See further G. K. Beale, *The Temple and the Church's Mission: A Biblical Theology of the Dwelling Place of God*, New Studies in Biblical Theology (Downers Grove, IL: IVP Academic, 2004); and James M. Hamilton Jr., *God's Indwelling Presence: The Holy Spirit in the Old and New Testaments*, New American Commentary Studies in Bible and Theology (Nashville: Broadman, 2006).

Redeemed from slavery, the church has received the fulfillment of divine instruction from the holy mountain in the sermon Jesus preached (Matthew 5–7), giving the church a new and better law: the law of Christ (1 Cor. 9:21; Gal. 6:2). Believers united to Christ by faith and immersed in the waters (Rom. 6:1–11; Gal. 3:26–29; Col. 2:11–13) have experienced the fulfillment of the crossing of the Red Sea (1 Cor. 10:2). As they partake of the Lord's Supper they are sustained by the fulfillment of the manna from heaven and water from the rock (1 Cor. 10:3–4; John 6:53–54; 7:37–39). They are liberated exiles (1 Pet. 1:1) who have girded up the loins of their minds (1 Pet. 1:13), to make their pilgrimage to the new and better land of promise, the lasting city with foundations (Heb. 11:10; 13:14), the new Jerusalem in the new heaven and the new earth (Revelation 21–22).

In the New Testament's typological presentation of the fulfillment of the Old Testament's anticipation, the *already* aspect of the salvation that Christ has accomplished has inaugurated a wilderness sojourn that puts believers on the way to the *not yet* consummation in the new and better land of promise, the new heavens and the new earth. We await the fulfillment of the conquest of the land (Revelation 19), when the new and better Joshua will give rest to the land (Heb. 4:8; Revelation 21–22).

The instructions about work we examine in this chapter are given to those who find the story of their lives in this drama of redemption: those who were slaves to sin but who have been liberated by the new and better Passover, who have been buried with Christ in baptism and raised to walk in new life, and who now sojourn toward the promised land, sustained by the very body and blood of the one who gave himself for our redemption. Between the cross and the new creation, the New Testament gives everything needed to please God in the work we do on the way.

Redeemed Work

We will take Romans 12:1–2 as an organizing principle for this discussion. Paul's instructions are based on the fact that the death and resurrection of Jesus liberates Christians from idolatrous approaches to work and motivates work unto the Lord that adorns the gospel. Paul writes in Romans 12:1–2:

> I appeal to you therefore, brothers, by the mercies of God, to present your bodies as a living sacrifice, holy and acceptable to God, which is your spiritual worship. Do not be conformed to this world, but be transformed by the renewal of your mind, that by testing you may discern what is the will of God, what is good and acceptable and perfect.

These words wave like a banner over every aspect of the Christian life, including the time and effort we put into the vocations God has given to us. Paul bases his appeal in Romans 12:1 on God's mercy. Because of the mercy of God that Paul has so eloquently described in Romans 1–11, he instructs believers to offer themselves as living sacrifices intended to please God. The believer no longer kills a sacrificial beast and hands it to the priest (cf. Lev. 1:4–8). Now the believer is both priest and (living!) sacrifice. In Romans 12:2 Paul tells his audience how to live this out, urging them not to be conformed to the world but to be transformed by renewal of the mind so as to know God's good, acceptable, and perfect will.

The concepts in Romans 12:1–2 energize everything the New Testament says about work. We will begin with the idea of conformity to the world, and we will approach this through a survey of New Testament statements. The first set of instructions we examine addresses what Christians *are not* to do with relationship to work. In each case, the forbidden behavior fails to reflect God's character and can be traced to idolatrous impulses (see Col. 3:5). From there we will move to a second set of statements, surveying New Testament perspectives on work that guide the behavior of those whose minds have been renewed. These tell Christians what it looks like to offer oneself as a living sacrifice when doing work. Both sets of statements enable followers of Jesus to live out the two greatest commandments: to love God with all we are and our neighbors as ourselves.

Living Christianly is not complicated, though it is profound (and exceedingly difficult!). The simplicity flows from the fact that everything commanded comes down to loving God and neighbor, while everything forbidden can be traced back to the worship of false gods, which places some other god before the Lord. There is, of course, frustration and what sometimes feels like inexplicability in our persistent failure to attain to God's glory (see Romans 7). So often this flows from failure to worship God, a failure revealed by our sin. When we sin, we seek gratification in a kind of worship, but worship of what is unworthy. Our thoughts, desires, actions, and habits reveal what we love, what we desire, and ultimately what we want to worship in order to find satisfaction.

Before turning to what we should do, we consider New Testament instruction on how *not* to work.

CONFORMITY TO THE WORLD: IDOLATROUS WORK

What would it look like to be an idolater at work? Let's begin with a summary of what it would *not* look like from what we saw in chapters 1 and 2. It would not look like:

- someone imaging forth the character of the one true and living God.
- someone exercising God-blessed dominion over the God-created world.

- someone ruling and subduing the earth as God commanded.
- someone flourishing in a futile and fallen world by eating, drinking, and enjoying their work.[2]

In short, idolatrous work would not look Christlike.

What *would* it look like? We can get a good idea of what idolatrous work would look like from what Paul tells people *not* to do in relationship to work. We will walk through this sampling of statements Paul makes in the order they appear in the New Testament.

EPHESIANS 4:28

Having described the spiritual blessings believers enjoy in Christ in Ephesians 1–3 (Eph. 1:3), Paul instructs Christians to walk in a manner worthy of their calling in Ephesians 4–6 (4:1). Christians are to live as though the Creator of the universe has redeemed them by the blood of his Son, freed them from sin, and promised that they will inherit the world with Abraham. Because he has (Eph. 1:3–14).

Paul's commands apply the Christian's new identity in Christ to life. The storyline sketched in the beginning of this chapter shapes and informs the Christian's identity. What Paul is doing, in essence, is articulating propositional truths that flow from the storyline. Just as Old Testament commandments reflected the way Israel was to live out God's righteousness in light of his redemptive work, New Testament commandments reflect the way the church is to live out God's righteousness in light of his redemptive work.

In the midst of these instructions, Paul writes in Ephesians 4:28, "Let the thief no longer steal, but rather let him labor, doing honest work with his own hands, so that he may have something to

---

2. Cf. Richard Lints, *Identity and Idolatry: The Image of God and Its Inversion*, New Studies in Biblical Theology (Downers Grove, IL: IVP Academic, 2015), 35.

share with anyone in need." The "not this/but that" instruction is an instance of the "put off/put on" instruction Paul began in 4:22–24 and continues through 4:32. Paul summarizes his commands to the Ephesians by saying, "Therefore be imitators of God, as beloved children" (5:1). The foundation of Ephesians 4:28, then, is that God is not a thief but a worker who is generous with the fruits of his labor. To bear his image as Christlike imitators of God, Christians must reflect the one they worship in the way they work.

In Ephesians 4:28 Paul condemns at least three things that do not reflect God's character:

- Theft (covetousness)
- Dishonest work (including all immoral, life-destroying schemes to make money)
- Selfishness (unwillingness to share)

The command to thieves that they are to steal no longer rearticulates the eighth commandment, "You shall not steal" (Ex. 20:15), in the new-covenant context.

Many see the Ten Commandments as umbrella-statement summaries of the broader teaching of the laws of Moses, and this is precisely the way the Westminster Larger Catechism's exposition interprets them. The Westminster Larger Catechism's explanation of the duties required and sins forbidden by the eighth commandment provides a thorough summary and exposition of this aspect of biblical teaching:

Q. 141. *What are the duties required in the eighth commandment?*
A. The duties required in the eighth commandment are, truth, faithfulness, and justice in contracts and commerce between man and man; rendering to every one his due; restitution of

goods unlawfully detained from the right owners thereof; giving and lending freely, according to our abilities, and the necessities of others; moderation of our judgments, wills, and affections concerning worldly goods; a provident care and study to get, keep, use, and dispose these things which are necessary and convenient for the sustentation of our nature, and suitable to our condition; a lawful calling, and diligence in it; frugality; avoiding unnecessary lawsuits, and suretiship, or other like engagements; and an endeavor, by all just and lawful means, to procure, preserve, and further the wealth and outward estate of others, as well as our own.

Q. 142. *What are the sins forbidden in the eighth commandment?*

A. The sins forbidden in the eighth commandment, besides the neglect of the duties required, are, theft, robbery, manstealing, and receiving anything that is stolen; fraudulent dealing, false weights and measures, removing landmarks, injustice and unfaithfulness in contracts between man and man, or in matters of trust; oppression, extortion, usury, bribery, vexatious lawsuits, unjust enclosures and depredation; engrossing commodities to enhance the price; unlawful callings, and all other unjust or sinful ways of taking or withholding from our neighbor what belongs to him, or of enriching ourselves; covetousness; inordinate prizing and affecting worldly goods; distrustful and distracting cares and studies in getting, keeping, and using them; envying at the prosperity of others; as likewise idleness, prodigality, wasteful gaming; and all other ways whereby we do unduly prejudice our own outward estate, and defrauding ourselves of the due use and comfort of that estate which God hath given us.

The Ephesians 4:28 command not to steal but labor with honest work hints at all that is implied by the eighth commandment. Paul essentially tells us we are not to rip people off. The instruction to do honest work prohibits immoral and life-destroying work; it means Christians should not work in the sin industries, whether those involve sexual immorality or are designed to addict people to substances or enslave them financially. And the purpose clause at the end of Ephesians 4:28 shows that we are not to be working merely for ourselves but for the good of others. The basic idea can be captured in one word: *integrity*.

How does this command prohibit idolatrous actions? To steal is to declare that you do not believe that the God of the Bible will keep his word to provide for those who trust him and punish those who break his commands. Theft becomes an option for one who thinks that God cannot be trusted to provide what is needed or desired, so he is not to be honored. The person who steals does not identify with the redeemed Israelites making pilgrimage through the wilderness lacking nothing because God provides. Instead, the thief exalts himself and his desire over God and the people being robbed, inverting the two great commandments. To engage in dishonest work is to proclaim that you don't think God will punish those who defraud others, commit adultery, or provoke covetousness. To refuse to share is to refuse to image forth the character of the generous God who is the giver of every good gift.

1 Thessalonians 4:11–12

Paul's comments to the Thessalonians indicate that some in the church did not want to live out their identity in Christ. Rather than reflecting the character of God by employing themselves in useful labor, they seem to have preferred doing nothing. This would explain why Paul repeatedly told them to get to work. In 1 Thessalonians

4:11–12 Paul instructed, "Aspire to live quietly, and to mind your own affairs, and to work with your hands, as we instructed you, so that you may walk properly before outsiders and be dependent on no one."

Paul's words here prohibit five fruits of avoiding work:

- Disruptive discontent
- Meddlesome behavior
- Laziness
- Disreputable conduct
- Dependence on others

The instruction "to aspire to live quietly" (4:11) means that Christians are not to cause the kinds of disturbances and disruptions that would attract negative attention to the faith. Similarly, the call to "mind your own affairs" (4:11) means that they are not to meddle in what does not concern them. The command to "work with your hands" (4:11) prohibits laziness, and their need to "walk properly before outsiders" (4:12) exhorts them to give Christianity a good reputation, not a bad one. Paul's view is that work is a good thing, and that under normal circumstances (barring things such as handicap, sickness, or aged decrepitude) people have a responsibility to provide for themselves and not burden others; thus the instruction to "be dependent on no one" (4:12). There is no place for a Christian who can work but chooses not to on the expectation that others will provide for him.

By embracing the wider story in which they were to find their identity, they were to find the quiet life desirable, their own affairs special assignments from God, the work they could do with their hands a privilege, and the productive pursuit of good repute with those outside a matter of building God's own reputation.

1 Thessalonians 5:14

Paul writes in 1 Thessalonians 5:14, "We urge you, brothers, admonish the idle, encourage the fainthearted, help the weak, be patient with them all." Here Paul charges the church to address four points where they are insufficient:

- Idleness
- Faintheartedness/timidity
- Weakness
- Unconcern for those who won't work

Idleness, faintheartedness, weakness, and unconcern do not characterize the God of the Bible. To be idle is to indulge the vice of sloth. To be fainthearted is the opposite of bold trust. Weakness and unconcern are polar opposites of the strength of character and long-suffering that mark those who know God.

The admonishment, encouragement, help, and patience that Paul calls for here is the opposite of indifference. In order for Christians to do these things, they will have to pay attention to one another, know one another, and then engage one another. Paul does not want Christians to be idle but active at work, not fainthearted and timid but bold and courageous, not weak but strong, and not piqued but patient.

2 Thessalonians 3:6–15

The idleness, meddlesomeness, and burdensome mooching that Paul addressed in 1 Thessalonians had evidently persisted in some who proved unrepentant, so Paul goes after these issues again in 2 Thessalonians 3:6–15:

> Now we command you, brothers, in the name of our Lord Jesus Christ, that you keep away from any brother who is walking in idleness and not in accord with the tradition that

you received from us. For you yourselves know how you ought to imitate us, because we were not idle when we were with you, nor did we eat anyone's bread without paying for it, but with toil and labor we worked night and day, that we might not be a burden to any of you. It was not because we do not have that right, but to give you in ourselves an example to imitate. For even when we were with you, we would give you this command: If anyone is not willing to work, let him not eat. For we hear that some among you walk in idleness, not busy at work, but busybodies. Now such persons we command and encourage in the Lord Jesus Christ to do their work quietly and to earn their own living.

As for you, brothers, do not grow weary in doing good. If anyone does not obey what we say in this letter, take note of that person, and have nothing to do with him, that he may be ashamed. Do not regard him as an enemy, but warn him as a brother.

Note the pitfalls Paul addresses here:

- Idleness (v. 6)
- Rejecting apostolic teaching (v. 6)
- Rejecting apostolic example (v. 7)
- Mooching (v. 8)
- Burdening (v. 8)
- Meddlesome busybodying (v. 11)
- Tolerance of what dishonors God (vv. 14–15)

In 2 Thessalonians 3:6 Paul regards the choice not to work but to be idle as a rejection of apostolic tradition. We should observe here that the opposite of idleness is not necessarily something that gives you a paycheck. It is possible, after all, to receive a paycheck even though you are basically idle. The kind of "work" that is the opposite of idleness is a diligent application of your capacities and faculties to the garden in which God has placed you (or to helping the gardener to whom God gave you) whether that be your home, your classroom, your workplace, or your field (literal or metaphorical).

These instructions reflect the wider biblical story, in which man and woman are made in God's image, endowed with significance and capacity. Consider the majesty of those made in the image and likeness of God. Shakespeare put these words about humanity on the lips of Hamlet:

> What a piece of work is man!
> How noble in reason!
> How infinite in faculties!
> In form and moving, how express and admirable!
> In action, how like an angel!
> In apprehension, how like a god!
> The beauty of the world!
> The paragon of animals! (2.2.2.301–307)

Along these lines, David Brooks cites a scholar who "writes that the human mind can take in 11 million pieces of information at any given moment. The most generous estimate is that people can be consciously aware of forty of these."[3] These considerations are relevant because God did not make man to be idle. Moreover, Paul has evidently entrusted to the Thessalonians a "tradition" that included the notion that God made them to be about the tasks to which he called them.

Not only are some Thessalonians out of accord with that apostolic tradition in verse 6; they are also out of accord with apostolic example in verse 7. Paul notes in verse 8 that he paid for what he ate and in verse 9

---

3. David Brooks, *The Social Animal: The Hidden Sources of Love, Character, and Achievement* (New York: Random House, 2011), x.

states that this was to set an example for the Thessalonians. Then he asserts in verse 10 that the Thessalonians are not to feed those who will not work, before urging people in verse 11 to work quietly and earn their own bread. Those who refuse this teaching should be warned as brothers (3:15), and if they persist in unrepentant idleness they are to be shamed by the church's having nothing to do with them (3:14).

Christians are not to be idle.

JAMES 5:4

Before we turn to consider the positive message of the kind of work that adorns the gospel, we should note the condemnation in James 5:4 of those who refuse to pay workers: "Behold, the wages of the laborers who mowed your fields, which you kept back by fraud, are crying out against you, and the cries of the harvesters have reached the ears of the Lord of hosts." To refuse to pay those who have worked for you is to exalt your own concerns—for your own interests, your own love for your money—over any other concerns: for justice, for those who have done honest work, or for the God who keeps watch over all transactions.

Work that does not communicate love for God and neighbor is idolatrous because such work exalts something other than God as ultimate, making a god of oneself or mammon or one's agenda or whatever. To put something other than God in God's place is to make an idol.

How do we avoid idolatrous approaches to work? To ask that question is to ask how to love God and neighbor in the way we work.

Renewal of Mind: Work unto the Lord That Adorns the Gospel

If the "do not be conformed to the world" side of the message comes down to avoiding idolatry, the "be transformed by the renewing of your mind" side amounts to love for God and neighbor. These principles are more than mere rules, for living out the human calling to image forth the true God by embodying his love can never be exhaustively codified.[4]

As a summary of the perspective of the New Testament authors on work, consider the following points that can be placed under the broad subheads of love for (1) God and (2) neighbor.

Work as an Expression of Love for God

The following four principles from four New Testament passages provide a cross section of the New Testament's teaching on how to love God through our work.

1) *Work to please God: The parable of the talents (Matt. 25:14–30).* In the parable of the talents Matthew presents Jesus commending initiative, diligence, and even savvy attempts to earn interest on one's money (Matt. 25:20–23, 27). He likewise discourages a slothful, fearful failure to be fruitful (25:26–30).

2) *Do all for God's glory (1 Cor. 10:31).* First Corinthians 10:31 communicates Paul's view that all things should be done for God's glory. God created the world to fill it with his glory, and those who would make God's character known should join him by pursuing his renown whether eating, drinking, or doing anything else.

3) *Do all in Christ's name (Col. 3:17).* The name of Jesus is about the character and mission of Jesus. To work in the name of the Lord Jesus, then, is to work in a way that reflects his character and joins his mission. To put the character of Jesus on display is to be transformed into the image of the invisible God (2 Cor. 3:18; Col. 1:15). This means that for Paul to speak of working in Christ's name is another way for him to urge working for God's glory.

---

4. Cf. Charles Taylor, *A Secular Age* (Cambridge, MA: Belknap, 2007), 706, 742: "Christian faith can never be decanted into a fixed code," and "the network of agape puts first the gut-driven response to this person. This can't be reduced to a general rule."

4) *Work from your soul for the Lord (Col. 3:23).* In addition to working for God's glory, Paul instructs the Colossians to work from the soul (εκ ψυχης) for the Lord. This appears to mean that they should put all they are into their work rather than merely doing things to preserve appearances before men. Christians should employ their creative capacities and soul-deep energies as they seek to serve God in their work. With God's glory as our aim, nothing less will suffice.

God's saving love can make even bitter bondage an arena for the display of God's glory. Phillis Wheatley's owner/master testified of her, "Phillis was brought from *Africa* to *America*, in the Year 1761, between Seven and Eight Years of Age." She was "the first black American to publish a book," and the second American woman to publish one. Her 1773 *Poems on Various Subjects Religious and Moral* is a work of genius, all the more remarkable given Wheatley was only nineteen or twenty years old at its publication. The overwhelming power of God's love is articulated by Wheatley in her poem, "On Being Brought from AFRICA to AMERICA":[5]

> It was mercy brought me from my *Pagan* land,
> Taught my benighted soul to understand
> That there's a God, that there's a *Saviour* too:
> Once I redemption neither sought nor knew.
> Some view our sable race with scornful eye,
>   "Their colour is a diabolic die."
> Remember, *Christians, Negros*, black as *Cain*,
> May be refin'd, and join th' angelic train.

---

5. Phillis Wheatley, *The Collected Works of Phillis Wheatley*, ed. John Shields (New York: Oxford University Press, 1989), 6, 18, 229. The capitalization, spelling, and italics in the quotations are original. Cf. the discussion of this poem in Vincent Carretta, *Phillis Wheatley: Biography of a Genius in Bondage* (Athens, GA: University of Georgia Press, 2011), 30, 60, 63, 86, 170, esp. 61: "Wheatley repeatedly appropriates the values of Christianity to judge and find wanting hypocritical self-styled Christians of European descent."

Phillis Wheatley was brought to America on a slave ship, but her experience of God's love was such that she considered herself to have been brought to America by God's *mercy*. She seems to suggest that it was better for her to know God as a slave than to have remained in her homeland with no access to Christianity. Though a slave, she knew the Savior. The love of God breathes through her work.

In addition to working for the Lord, Christians should work to benefit other people.

WORK AS AN EXPRESSION OF LOVE FOR NEIGHBOR

The greatest commandment is to love the Lord our God, and the second is like it, to love our neighbor as ourselves. Following is a sampling of New Testament statements on how we work in order to love our neighbor.

1) *Following Paul's example of hard work to benefit others (1 Cor. 9:6–27; 15:10)*. In 1 Corinthians 9 Paul discusses the way that he did not make use of his rights but instead worked to pay his own way. He did this to benefit the Corinthians spiritually, and in so doing he was Christlike in that he sacrificed himself on their behalf.

In 1 Corinthians 15:10 Paul states that he worked hard, harder than the other apostles, though he notes that he did so by God's grace. Christians should follow Paul's example (11:1) on both points: we should sacrifice ourselves for the benefit of others, and we should pray for God's grace that we might work hard.

2) *To support the ministry (1 Cor. 9:14; Gal. 6:6)*. At various points in his letters Paul indicates that those who benefit from the message of the gospel should supply the financial and logistical needs for those who minister the gospel. This means that Christians should work so that they can benefit others who will enjoy the ministry of the gospel supported and made possible by the Christian workers who have generously given from the fruits of their labor.

3) *To share with the needy (Eph. 4:28)*. As we saw above, Paul exhorts the Ephesians to share with those in need. Christians should work so that they can support the ministry of the gospel and so that they can give charitably to those in need. In 1 Timothy 5:9–16 Paul gives instructions on the support of widows, including how to determine whether a widow qualifies for such support. The principles Paul articulates enable Christians to avoid funding the idleness of those who should be working (cf. 2 Thess. 3:6–15) or the irresponsibility of those who should be supporting members of their own family (1 Tim. 5:8, 16). Paul does not want Christians to help in ways that hurt.[6]

4) *To live an undisruptive life (1 Thess. 4:11; 2 Thess. 3:12)*. On the negative side is the instruction not to be disruptive, and on the positive side is the corresponding instruction to work so as to live a quiet life. The work we do is the grand project that occupies us: our opportunity to show the world what God is like as we image forth his character.

5) *As a good testimony for unbelievers (1 Cor. 9:12; 1 Thess. 4:12; 1 Tim. 5:14; 6:1; Titus 2:5, 9)*. At many points in his letters Paul instructs Christians to live in a way that reflects concern for how non-Christians will perceive Christianity and its adherents. That is to say, Christians are to work in ways that commend the faith to outsiders. Believers are to be winsome and attractive, not repulsive and obnoxious. This concern for how unbelievers perceive the faith is inextricably connected to a desire for others to know, enjoy, and glorify God in Christ. This aspect of doing good work links up with the Great Commission (Matt. 28:18–20). Christians contribute to the task of making disciples of all nations by doing good work that gives the faith a good reputation.

---

6. See further Steve Corbett and Brian Fikkert, *When Helping Hurts: How to Alleviate Poverty Without Hurting the Poor . . . and Yourself*, rev. ed. (Chicago: Moody, 2012).

6) *Not to burden others (2 Cor. 11:9; 12:13, 14, 16; 1 Thess. 2:9; 4:12; 2 Thess. 3:8).* Rather than unduly burdening other members of the church, Christians should work so that they can contribute financially to the ministry of the gospel and the help of those in need.

7) *In brotherly love that transcends race and status (1 Tim. 6:2; Philem. 16).* The unity that believers enjoy in Christ overturns and transcends degrading cultural standards that exalt some people over others.[7] Christians are to work in ways that reflect the dignity and value of every human, as all are made in God's image. Further, those in the family of faith are to be regarded as brothers and treated as coheirs of Christ. Union with Christ by faith gives believers a new identity that is to be lived out already now in the context of work relationships that partake of the *not yet* aspects of this time between the times, before the full dawning of the age to come.

Work in Christ

Tim Keller writes, "Christians who grasp a biblical theology of work learn not only to value and participate in the work of all people but to also see ways to work distinctively as Christians."[8] As we wait for the redemption of our lowly bodies and resurrection from the dead, Christians are to work in ways that show love for God and neighbor. So doing will enable us to live out the image and likeness of the true and living God. We are, after all, being transformed from one degree of glory to another into the image of his Son (2 Cor. 3:18). Walking with God in this way will allow us to flourish in the midst of fallen futility.

---

7. For the way Paul's instructions on the Lord's Supper stand against worldly distinctions in the church, see James M. Hamilton Jr., "The Lord's Supper in Paul," in *The Lord's Supper*, ed. Thomas R. Schreiner and Matt Crawford, New American Commentary Studies in Bible and Theology (Nashville: Broadman, 2010), 68–102.

8. Timothy Keller, *Every Good Endeavor: Connecting Your Work to God's Work* (New York: Riverhead, 2014), 149.

4

Restoration

Work in the New Heavens and the New Earth

Wolfgang Amadeus Mozart is one of the most famous makers of music ever to live. He composed over six hundred pieces of music that are cherished and studied and known the world over to this day. Mozart died in 1791 when he was only thirty-five years old. His early death is one of the most tragic cases of lost genius in the history of humanity.

His work was cut short by an early death.

In the preface to the Pulitzer Prize–winning novel, *A Confederacy of Dunces* by John Kennedy Toole, Walker Percy writes, "It is a great pity that John Kennedy Toole is not alive and well and writing," having explained, "the tragedy of the book is the tragedy of the author—his suicide in 1969 at the age of thirty-two. Another tragedy is the body of work we have been denied."[1]

Toole's work was cut short by self-slaughter.

---

1. John Kennedy Toole, *A Confederacy of Dunces* (Baton Rouge: Louisiana State University Press, 1980), *xiii*.

What We Were Made to Do

This side of the sin at the Tree of Knowledge of Good and Evil, our work is ruined by all manner of afflictions moral, physical, emotional, and mental. How many athletes have had promising careers ended by injury? How many flourishing young debaters have been cut down by cancer? How many engineers can no longer do their work because of inexplicable seizures? How many moral failures have disqualified pastors, teachers, and politicians?

And even if a person enjoys a full three score and ten or more, the working years will pass into memory as, in the words of Ecclesiastes, "the almond tree blossoms, the grasshopper drags itself along, and desire fails, because man is going to his eternal home" when "the silver cord is snapped, or the golden bowl is broken, or the pitcher is shattered at the fountain, or the wheel broken at the cistern, and the dust returns to the earth as it was, and the spirit returns to God who gave it" (Eccles. 12:5–7).

Death will end our work. And if we live long enough, before death ends it, frailty will.

We have seen that God created man to work, to be fruitful and multiply and fill the earth, to subdue it, and to exercise dominion over the animal kingdom (Gen. 1:28), working and keeping the garden God made (2:15), imaging God's own character to improve God's creation so that all life—plant, animal, human—might flourish.

Man sinned, however, bringing death and futility into the world. God's merciful instructions enable us to flourish in fallen futility, and the redemption God accomplished in Christ frees us from idolatrous approaches to work and motivates us to work unto the Lord to adorn the gospel as our vocations become the arenas in which we love God and neighbor. In spite of all God has done, however, we are not what we were prior to sin, and the world has been subjected to futility. Where will this story arc land?

To ask that question is to ask what we can say about work after Christ returns to consummate redemption. What will work look like in the new heavens and the new earth?

We cannot be sure, of course, because God's way is to do what has never before been seen or imagined (cf. 1 Cor. 2:9). As Paul said, "For now we see in a mirror dimly, but then face to face. Now I know in part; then I shall know fully, even as I have been fully known" (1 Cor. 13:12).

We have, however, two kinds of information from which we can formulate conclusions about the perspective of the biblical authors on what awaits us. On the one hand, we have details found in particular statements about the future, and on the other hand, we have a broader picture in which these details are to be understood.

The broader picture takes its outline from the Old Testament expectation of a new exodus, new Sinai law, new temple, new experience of the Spirit, new pilgrimage through the wilderness, and new conquest of the land, which is a new Eden, all led by a new King from David's line. This fund of imagery is the account from which the New Testament draws when it shows the payoff of all that Jesus accomplished. This fund of imagery is also drawn on when the New Testament points to what Jesus will accomplish when he returns.

God will bring to pass the purposes he set out to achieve when he spoke the world into existence. God has not trashed his first failed attempt and started over. To the contrary, what he set out to do when he made this world he will bring about when he makes it new. God will make the world new, and we will do new work.

The new work we will do is the work of ruling and subduing, working and keeping, exercising dominion and rendering judgment, all as God's people in God's place in God's way.

We begin with a consideration of the raw data, a sampling of the details the Bible gives us about the future. From there we will turn to the broader picture against which those details make sense. So we begin by looking at particular trees; then we back away to see the forest those trees form. Or to change the metaphor, we begin with the building blocks; then we look at the house constructed from them.

The Building Materials

What will the situation be like when God has accomplished all his purposes?[2] We find a description in Daniel 9:24: "Seventy weeks are decreed about your people and your holy city, to finish the transgression, to put an end to sin, and to atone for iniquity, to bring in everlasting righteousness, to seal both vision and prophet, and to anoint a most holy place." Seventy weeks of years would add up to 490 years. Every forty-nine years Israel celebrated the Jubilee, when the captives went free, debts were canceled, and the land reverted to those whose tribal inheritance it was. When the Jubilee came, a loud trumpet was sounded (Lev. 25:9), and Isaiah 27:13 indicates that the consummation of God's purposes will be marked by the blast of a great trumpet. Paul articulates the same idea in 1 Thessalonians 4:16. It appears, then, that the 490 years of Daniel 9:24's seventy weeks speak of a tenfold Jubilee, and at the completion of that symbolic period all of God's purposes will be realized.[3]

Daniel 9:24 tells us that there will be no more sin, there will be eternal righteousness, vision and prophet will be fulfilled, and a new temple will be anointed. The temple was a symbol of the world God made (see Ps. 78:69; Isa. 66:1), and in Revelation's depiction of the

---

2. For a thorough systematic discussion, see Herman Bavinck, *Reformed Dogmatics: Holy Spirit, Church, and New Creation*, vol. 4 (Grand Rapids, MI: Baker Academic, 2008), 715–30.

3. For further discussion, see chap. 5, "Seventy Weeks and Seventy Weeks of Years: Daniel's Prayer and Gabriel's Revelation," in my *With the Clouds of Heaven: The Book of Daniel in Biblical Theology*, New Studies in Biblical Theology (Downers Grove, IL: IVP Academic, 2014), 105–34.

New Jerusalem, John describes it as a new temple. This leads me to think that the anointed new holy place in Daniel 9:24 will be the cosmic temple of the new heavens and the new earth.

The idea that the consummation of all things will result in sinless righteousness is confirmed in 2 Peter 3:13: "But according to his promise we are waiting for new heavens and a new earth in which righteousness dwells." The new heavens and the new earth will be a new cosmic temple, and unlike what happened when the first Adam sinned, the second Adam, Jesus, will ensure that God's will is done when God's kingdom comes.

How will any sinners enter that kingdom? And if they do enter it, what will their responsibilities be? God made Adam as a *royal* figure, whose task it was to exercise dominion over God's world. God also made Adam as a *priestly* figure, whose job of working and keeping the garden is described with the same language used of the Levites who were to work and keep the tabernacle. Adam sinned and was expelled from the garden. Then God made Israel a "kingdom of priests" (Ex. 19:6) and offered them a new opportunity to live in his presence in the Land of Promise, almost a new Eden. Just as Adam sinned and was expelled, Israel broke the covenant and was expelled.

Jesus came as Israel's *king* from the line of David and as the prophesied *priest* according to the order of Melchizedek, and because he succeeded where Israel failed, John writes in Revelation 1:5–6, "To him who loves us and has freed us from our sins by his blood and made us a *kingdom, priests* to his God and Father, to him be glory and dominion forever and ever. Amen." The people of Jesus are a "royal priesthood" (1 Pet. 2:9), made to exercise dominion and worship God, mediating the knowledge of God to all creation.

How do we get from these ideas to work in the new heaven and the new earth? In this way: between here and there is the resurrection.

Resurrection

The Old and New Testaments point to an embodied future for the righteous and the wicked. The quintessential Old Testament statement of this idea is Daniel 12:2: "Many of those who sleep in the dust of the earth shall awake, some to everlasting life, and some to shame and everlasting contempt" (see also Isa. 25:7–8; 26:14–19).[4]

Humanity's future is not a disembodied, unearthly existence. We will be raised from the dead and granted resurrection bodies, as Paul says in Philippians 3:20–21: "Our citizenship is in heaven, and from it we await a Savior, the Lord Jesus Christ, who will transform our lowly body to be like his glorious body, by the power that enables him even to subject all things to himself."

The resurrection of the body joins with the hope for a new heaven and a new earth. The experiments in social engineering that history has seen are trying to bring about God's kingdom by man's power. Whittaker Chambers, who recounted his journey into and out of communism in his book, *Witness*, put this forcefully:

> The communist vision is the vision of Man without God. It is the vision of man's mind displacing God as the creative intelligence of the world. It is the vision of man's liberated mind, by the sole force of its rational intelligence, redirecting man's destiny and reorganizing man's life and the world. . . . The Communist Party has posed in practical form the most revolutionary question in history: God or Man?[5]

---

4. For a biblical theological exposition of the pentateuchal roots of resurrection, see Mitchell L. Chase, "Resurrection Hope in Daniel 12:2: An Exercise in Biblical Theology," PhD dissertation, The Southern Baptist Theological Seminary, 2013; Chase, "From Dust You Shall Arise: Resurrection Hope in the Old Testament," *Southern Baptist Journal of Theology* 18, no. 4 (2014): 9–29; and Chase, "The Genesis of Resurrection Hope: Exploring Its Early Presence and Deep Roots," *Journal of the Evangelical Theological Society* 57 (2014): 467–80.

5. Whittaker Chambers, *Witness*, 50th anniversary ed. (Washington, DC: Regnery, 2001), 9–10.

Charles Taylor discusses the dilemmas that both Christians and secularists face, tensions between not mutilating our humanity in attempts to deny bodily impulses to sex or violence in order to achieve some good while not sanitizing or whitewashing how bad things really are in the world.[6] The desire not to mutilate oneself is at work in the thinking of the Uber driver with whom I conversed as he drove me to the airport recently. He explained that he left Christianity because he had to be himself. He identifies as gay, and he viewed the mortification of what the Bible identifies as sinful desire as mutilating, so he left the faith.

The biblical hope for resurrection from the dead makes any self-denial the Bible imposes a worthwhile sacrifice given what we stand to gain, and the renovation of the heavens and the earth promises that every wrong (including disordered desires) will be put right. In her novel *Gilead*, Marilynne Robinson's Reverend John Ames puts it well: "'He will wipe the tears from all faces [Rev. 21:4; Isa. 25:8].' It takes nothing from the loveliness of the verse to say that is exactly what will be required."[7]

Many texts in the Bible speak not only of the resurrection of the dead but of the restoration of the years the locusts have eaten (Joel 2:25), indicating that God will restore what has been ruined and lost because of sin. We have every reason to believe that God will satisfy every longing he built into the human heart. Longings for sinful things are but perversions of righteous desires. God will satisfy us.

RESTORATION

The restoration pertains to people and land.

Of people. The restoration of the people simply fleshes out the

---

6. Charles Taylor, *A Secular Age* (Cambridge, MA: Belknap, 2007), 639–42.
7. Marilynne Robinson, *Gilead: A Novel* (New York: Picador, 2006), 246.

hope for resurrection discussed in the previous section. I remember years ago watching a dear blind friend of mine sing in the choir of the Lord's great salvation. As I watched him rejoicing in the Lord, I thought to myself: that man is going to see someday. I can say that because of Isaiah 29:18: "In that day the deaf shall hear the words of a book, and out of their gloom and darkness the eyes of the blind shall see." We find the same ideas in Isaiah 35:5–6: "Then the eyes of the blind shall be opened, and the ears of the deaf unstopped; then shall the lame man leap like a deer, and the tongue of the mute sing for joy." Anticipating the great restoration, Jesus came giving sight to the blind and making the lame whole.

In the context of Isaiah, these texts point to the reversal of the hardening Isaiah was commissioned to administer in Isaiah 6:9–10. The lifting of that hardening and the restoration of the people is bound up with the resurrection from the dead, as Paul says in Romans 11:15: "What will their acceptance mean but life from the dead?" (on the hardening, see Rom. 11:25–32). Paul describes the restoration we long for when he declares, "We shall also bear the image of the man of heaven" (1 Cor. 15:49).

Of land. God's ultimate plan is a glorious eschatological restoration. That means things will be put back as they were before being defiled, and we can expect the restoration to be better than the original. The idea that God will bring about a new and better Eden is articulated in Isaiah 51:3:

> For the LORD comforts Zion;
> > he comforts all her waste places
> and makes her wilderness like Eden,
> > her desert like the garden of the LORD;
> joy and gladness will be found in her,
> > thanksgiving and the voice of song.

Ezekiel 36:35 is similar: "They will say, 'This land that was desolate has become like the garden of Eden, and the waste and desolate and ruined cities are now fortified and inhabited.'" When God restores his people, the fallen booth of David will be raised up, ruins rebuilt as of old (Amos 9:11). God's people will possess the land (9:12), which will be so fertile the harvest will continue until the time to replant (9:13). The fortunes of the people will be restored (9:14), and the people will be planted in the land never to be uprooted (9:15).

Raised from the dead and restored, but for what? What will God's people do in resurrected bodies in the new creation?

INHERIT, STEWARD, REIGN, AND JUDGE

Jesus promised in Matthew 5:5, "Blessed are the meek, for they shall inherit the earth." God put Adam in the earth to fill and subdue it. Adam forfeited dominion over the land to the Serpent when he sinned; thus Jesus spoke of Satan as the ruler of this world (John 12:31). God promised land to Abraham (Gen. 12:1–3), then gave land to Israel—land they forfeited when they broke the covenant. By casting out this world's ruler (John 12:31), Jesus reclaimed his rightful dominion over the earth. He is the son of man from Daniel 7 who will exercise everlasting dominion (Dan. 7:14), and his saints will possess the kingdom and reign with him (7:22, 27).

Jesus gave some indication of how the faithful will be rewarded when, speaking of a master who set a servant over his household to feed them, he said, "Blessed is that servant whom his master will find so doing when he comes. Truly, I say to you, he will set him over all his possessions" (Matt. 24:46–47; cf. Luke 12:43–44). These words point in the direction of Jesus making those faithful to him stewards over all that belongs to him. This teaching of Jesus may stand behind Paul's telling the Corinthians, "So let no one boast in men. For all things are yours, whether Paul or Apollos or Cephas or the world or life or death or the present or the future—all are yours, and you are Christ's, and Christ is God's" (1 Cor. 3:21–23).

God put Adam in the garden as a royal priest. Jesus the priest-king conquered where Adam failed, and Jesus made his people a royal priesthood. Jesus also promises to give the priest-kings who follow him responsibility. In Matthew's account of the rich young ruler "Jesus said to them, 'Truly, I say to you, in the new world, when the Son of Man will sit on his glorious throne, you who have followed me will also sit on twelve thrones, judging the twelve tribes of Israel'" (Matt. 19:28). This being a statement made to the Twelve, with the reference to twelve thrones, it does not necessarily mean that every last one of Jesus's followers will be so seated. Still, it does indicate that followers of Jesus will exercise the dominion initially entrusted to Adam.

The same idea can be found in the parable of the talents. The master says to the ones who multiplied what was entrusted to them, "Well done, good and faithful servant. You have been faithful over a little; I will set you over much" (Matt. 25:21, 23). Luke presents a similar parable of ten minas in which the faithful are told, "Well done, good servant! Because you have been faithful in a very little, you shall have authority over ten cities" (Luke 19:17; cf. 19:19).

Because the throne was associated with judgment in the ancient world, the teaching of Jesus that his followers would have authority and reign again backgrounds what Paul wrote to the Corinthians: "Or do you not know that the saints will judge the world? And if the world is to be judged by you, are you incompetent to try trivial cases? Do you not know that we are to judge angels?" (1 Cor. 6:2–3).

The four living creatures not only praise Jesus in Revelation 5:9 for ransoming people from every tribe and language and people and nation; they go on to say in 5:10, "You have made them a kingdom and priests to our God, and they shall reign on the earth."

Under King Jesus, the new heavens and the new earth will be

ruled by those who exercise the dominion that he reclaimed, those whom he made a kingdom and priests. These are also those who will feast with Jesus.

FEAST

Jesus said in Matthew 8:11, "I tell you, many will come from east and west and recline at table with Abraham, Isaac, and Jacob in the kingdom of heaven." Then as he instituted the Lord's Supper, Jesus asserted, "I tell you I will not drink again of this fruit of the vine until that day when I drink it new with you in my Father's kingdom" (Matt. 26:29).

This feast will be for the faithful. In Luke 22:28–30 Jesus says, "You are those who have stayed with me in my trials, and I assign to you, as my Father assigned to me, a kingdom, that you may eat and drink at my table in my kingdom and sit on thrones judging the twelve tribes of Israel."

The feast will accompany the marriage of the Lamb (Rev. 19:7), as John relates in Revelation 19:9: "The angel said to me, 'Write this: Blessed are those who are invited to the marriage supper of the Lamb.' And he said to me, 'These are the true words of God.'" Blessed indeed will be all who rejoice at the marriage feast of the Lamb.

Faithfulness now guarantees future reward, and future reward motivates faithfulness now. This is why Paul concludes his discussion of the resurrection in 1 Corinthians 15 with the words, "Therefore, my beloved brothers, be steadfast, immovable, always abounding in the work of the Lord, knowing that in the Lord your labor is not in vain" (1 Cor. 15:58; cf. "vain" in 15:2, 14, 17).

The House They Build

What forest does this collection of trees form? What house do these materials construct?

The correspondences between Eden and the tabernacle and the temple indicate that God set out to make a cosmic temple when he built the world. That temple was to be guarded and served, worked and kept, by the image and likeness of God. Instead of working and keeping, Adam allowed the Serpent into the garden, listened to his lies, and forfeited dominion to Satan. As a result, none of Adam's children got to live in Eden.

Jesus cast out Satan by going to the cross, and when he returns he will set in motion the events of the end that will culminate in the heavens and the earth becoming what God originally built them to be: a cosmic temple. In that cosmic temple, the people who belong to Jesus, who have been transformed into his image, will rule and subdue, work and keep, and no snake will ever enter that garden to speak lies to the bride of Christ. Jesus himself will ensure the safety of that redeemed place.

The details not only allow us to sketch a picture of the place; we can also see a repeated typological pattern that culminates in the triumphant reign of Christ:

- Adam in the garden to work it and keep it and cause it to fill the earth.
- Israel in the land to work it and keep it and expand its boundaries.
- The church in the world to make disciples of all nations.
- Jesus returning to make the world his kingdom.

God put Adam in the garden for him to live and work there. He sinned and was expelled.

God put Israel in the land for them to live and work there. They sinned and were expelled.

The church is in the world to live and work, redeemed by Jesus but still subject to decay.

Jesus will come and raise the dead. Jesus will come and cleanse the land. Jesus will come and banish sin. Jesus will come and make weapons and gates and locks and alarm systems unnecessary. Jesus will come and make it so that mankind can do the work in the world that God created us to do.

Conclusion

I remember one of my teachers reflecting on his vocation as an instructor. He got a far-off look in his eye as he mused on the way he felt when he walked into the classroom, his whole being resonating with the words: "I was made for this hour."

God built us to do something, and in the new heavens and the new earth we will be liberated to do the work for which God fitted us when he formed us in the womb.

We can scarcely imagine it, but everything that makes work miserable here will be removed. All our sinful concerns about ourselves will be swallowed up in devotion to the one we serve. All our frustration that we have to be doing *this* task, not *that* other one we prefer, will be abolished because of our experience of the one who gave us the assignment. All inclination to evil will have been removed from our hearts, so we will enjoy the freedom of wanting to obey, wanting to serve, wanting to do right. And the right that we have to do will no more be in conflict with needing time with kids or friends or spouse, because we will have forever. Never again will we fear that our work is futile, vain, monotonous, or meaningless, because we will see clearly that the significance of our work springs from the one we serve.

God will be everything to us. We will serve him with whole and complete hearts.

The prophesied new exodus will have been completed. Our pilgrimage through the wilderness will be over. Our new and better Joshua will have conquered the land. We will enter that good land to live in God's presence, and we will enjoy the blessings of the covenant in the world without end.

In such a place under such a king, we who were created to work will finally be doing what we were made to do. Sin and frustrations removed. Death no more. Jesus will keep the snakes out of the city.

The closing lines of J. R. R. Tolkien's poem "Mythopoeia" speak to the glories that await those who belong to the Lord Jesus:

> In Paradise they look no more awry;
> and though they make anew, they make no lie.
> Be sure they still will make, not being dead,
> and poets shall have flames upon their head,
> and harps whereon their faultless fingers fall:
> there each shall choose for ever from the All.[1]

---

1. J. R. R. Tolkien, *Tree and Leaf: Including "Mythopoeia"* (London: HarperCollins, 2001), 90.

For Further Reading

Alexander, T. Desmond. "Genealogies, Seed, and the Compositional Unity of Genesis." *Tyndale Bulletin* 44 (1993): 255–70.

Bavinck, Herman. *Reformed Dogmatics. Vol. 4, Holy Spirit, Church, and New Creation.* Grand Rapids, MI: Baker Academic, 2008.

Beale, G. K. *The Temple and the Church's Mission: A Biblical Theology of the Dwelling Place of God.* New Studies in Biblical Theology. Downers Grove, IL: IVP Academic, 2004.

Beckwith, Roger T. *The Old Testament Canon of the New Testament Church and Its Background in Early Judaism.* Grand Rapids, MI: Eerdmans, 1985.

Brooks, David. *The Social Animal: The Hidden Sources of Love, Character, and Achievement.* New York: Random House, 2011.

Burk, Denny. *What Is the Meaning of Sex?* Wheaton, IL: Crossway, 2013.

Burk, Denny, and Heath Lambert. *Transforming Homosexuality: What the Bible Says about Sexual Orientation and Change.* Phillipsburg, NJ: P&R, 2015.

Carretta, Vincent. *Phillis Wheatley: Biography of a Genius in Bondage.* Athens, GA: University of Georgia Press, 2011.

Chambers, Whittaker. *Witness.* 50th anniversary ed. Washington, DC: Regnery, 2001.

Chase, Mitchell L. "From Dust You Shall Arise: Resurrection Hope in the Old Testament." *Southern Baptist Journal of Theology* 18, no. 4 (2014): 9–29.

———. "The Genesis of Resurrection Hope: Exploring Its Early Presence and Deep Roots." *Journal of the Evangelical Theological Society* 57 (2014): 467–80.

———. "Resurrection Hope in Daniel 12:2: An Exercise in Biblical Theology." PhD dissertation, The Southern Baptist Theological Seminary, 2013.

Cole, Robert L. *Psalms 1–2: Gateway to the Psalter*. Sheffield, UK: Sheffield Phoenix Press, 2013.

Collins, Jack. "A Syntactical Note (Genesis 3:15): Is the Woman's Seed Singular or Plural?" *Tyndale Bulletin* 48 (1997): 139–48.

Corbett, Steve, and Brian Fikkert. *When Helping Hurts: How to Alleviate Poverty Without Hurting the Poor . . . and Yourself*. Revised ed. Chicago: Moody, 2012.

Dempster, Stephen G. *Dominion and Dynasty: A Biblical Theology of the Hebrew Bible*. New Studies in Biblical Theology. Downers Grove, IL: IVP Academic, 2003.

Emadi, Samuel Cyrus. "Covenant, Typology, and the Story of Joseph: A Literary-Canonical Examination of Genesis 37–50." PhD dissertation, The Southern Baptist Theological Seminary, 2016.

Girgis, Sherif, Robert George, and Ryan T. Anderson. "What Is Marriage?" *Harvard Journal of Law and Public Policy* 34 (2010): 245–87.

Grudem, Wayne. *Evangelical Feminism and Biblical Truth: An Analysis of More Than 100 Disputed Questions*. Sisters, OR: Multnomah, 2004.

Hamilton, James M, Jr. "A Biblical Theology of Motherhood." *Journal of Discipleship and Family Ministry* 2, no. 2 (2012): 6–13.

———. *Exalting Jesus in Ezra and Nehemiah*. Christ-Centered Exposition. Nashville: Broadman, 2014.

———. "Gender Roles and the Glory of God: A Sermon on 1 Corinthians 11:2–12." *Journal for Biblical Manhood and Womanhood* 9 (2004): 35–39.

———. *God's Glory in Salvation through Judgment: A Biblical Theology*. Wheaton, IL: Crossway, 2010.

———. *God's Indwelling Presence: The Holy Spirit in the Old and New Testaments*. New American Commentary Studies in Bible and Theology. Nashville: Broadman, 2006.

———. "The Lord's Supper in Paul." In *The Lord's Supper*, edited by Thomas R. Schreiner and Matt Crawford, 68–102. New American Commentary Studies in Bible and Theology. Nashville: Broadman, 2010.

———. "Original Sin in Biblical Theology." In *Adam, the Fall, and Original Sin: Theological, Biblical, and Scientific Perspectives*, edited by Hans Madueme and Michael Reeves, 189–208. Grand Rapids, MI: Baker Academic, 2014.

———. "The Seed of the Woman and the Blessing of Abraham." *Tyndale Bulletin* 58 (2007): 253–73.

———. "The Skull Crushing Seed of the Woman: Inner-Biblical Interpretation of Genesis 3:15." *The Southern Baptist Journal of Theology* 10, no. 2 (2006): 30–54.

———. *Song of Songs: A Biblical-Theological, Allegorical, Christological Interpretation*. Fearn, UK: Christian Focus, 2015.

———. "Was Joseph a Type of the Messiah? Tracing the Typological Identification between Joseph, David, and Jesus." *The Southern Baptist Journal of Theology* 12 (2008): 52–77.

———. *What Is Biblical Theology?* Wheaton, IL: Crossway, 2014.

———. "What Women Can Do in Ministry: Full Participation within Biblical Boundaries." In *Women, Ministry and the Gospel: Ex-*

ploring New Paradigms, edited by Mark Husbands and Timothy Larsen, 32–52. Downers Grove, IL: IVP Academic, 2007.

———. *With the Clouds of Heaven: The Book of Daniel in Biblical Theology*. New Studies in Biblical Theology. Downers Grove, IL: IVP Academic, 2014.

Hesiod. *The Homeric Hymns and Homerica*. Translated by Hugh G. Evelyn-White. LCL 57. Cambridge, MA: Harvard University Press, 1914.

Keller, Timothy. *Every Good Endeavor: Connecting Your Work to God's Work*. New York: Riverhead, 2014.

Klink, Edward W., and Darian R. Lockett. *Understanding Biblical Theology: A Comparison of Theory and Practice*. Grand Rapids, MI: Zondervan, 2012.

Lints, Richard. *Identity and Idolatry: The Image of God and Its Inversion*. New Studies in Biblical Theology. Downers Grove, IL: IVP Academic, 2015.

Robinson, Marilynne. *Gilead: A Novel*. New York: Picador, 2006.

Schreiner, Thomas R., and Andreas J. Köstenberger. *Women in the Church: An Analysis and Application of 1 Timothy 2:9–15*. 2nd ed. Grand Rapids, MI: Baker Academic, 2005.

Smith, James K. A. *Desiring the Kingdom: Worship, Worldview, and Cultural Formation*. Grand Rapids, MI: Baker Academic, 2009.

Taylor, Charles. *A Secular Age*. Cambridge, MA: Belknap, 2007.

Tolkien, J. R. R. *Tree and Leaf: Including "Mythopoeia."* London: HarperCollins, 2001.

Ware, Bruce A., and John Starke, eds. *One God in Three Persons: Unity of Essence, Distinction of Persons, Implications for Life*. Wheaton, IL: Crossway, 2015.

Wenham, Gordon J. *The Psalter Reclaimed: Praying and Praising with the Psalms*. Wheaton, IL: Crossway, 2013.

———. "Sanctuary Symbolism in the Garden of Eden Story." In *I Studied Inscriptions from before the Flood: Ancient Near Eastern, Literary, and Linguistic Approaches to Genesis 1–11*, edited by Richard Hess and David Toshio Tsumara, 399–404. Winona Lake, IN: Eisenbrauns, 1994.

Wheatley, Phillis. *The Collected Works of Phillis Wheatley*. Edited by John Shields. New York: Oxford University Press, 1989.

Wifall, Walter. "Gen 3:15—A Protevangelium?" *Catholic Biblical Quarterly* 36 (1974): 361–65.

Wright, Addison G. "Additional Numerical Patterns in Qoheleth." *Catholic Biblical Quarterly* 45 (1983): 32–43.

———. "The Riddle of the Sphinx: The Structure of the Book of Qoheleth." *Catholic Biblical Quarterly* 30 (1968): 313–34.

———. "The Riddle of the Sphinx Revisited: Numerical Patterns in the Book of Qoheleth." *Catholic Biblical Quarterly* 42 (1980): 38–51.

General Index

Abel: comparison of to Cain, 45–48; as identified by his work, 44; as a keeper of sheep, 43

Abraham, God's promises to, 31, 32, 42, 58, 59, 69; passing down of to the descendants of Abraham, 31

Adam and Eve, 97; Adam as a priestly figure, 24, 93, 98; Adam as a royal figure, 93, 98; Adam's naming of Eve, 27, 38; as created in the image of God, 18, 19, 21, 22, 31; as created male and female, 19–20; marriage of, 20–21. *See also* fall, the; work in Eden; work in the very good creation, God's design for work (fill, subdue, exercise dominion)

Alexander, T. Desmond, 42n1

Anderson, Ryan T., 27n13

Bavinck, Herman, 92n2

Beale, G. K., 21n7, 71n1

Beckwith, Roger T., 12n3

biblical theology, 11–12; canonical approach to, 11–12, 11n1; and the history of redemption, 11, 11n2; incorporation of Old Testament Wisdom Literature into, 13; and narrative literature, 56; and worldview, 11, 11n2

"Big Rock Candy Mountain," 15–16

Brooks, David, 82

Burk, Denny, 26n11, 27n13

Cain: comparison of to Abel, 45–48; cursing of by God, 46; as a fugitive, 46–47; as identified by his work, 44; murder of Abel by as opposed to God's purposes for humanity, 46; as a seed of the Serpent, 46; and sin's desire, 35; as "a worker of the ground," 43–44, 46

Carretta, Vincent, 85n5

Chambers, Whittaker, 94

Chase, Mitchell L., 57n5, 94n4

church, the, 100; as the family of God, 55

Cole, Robert L., 17n3

Collins, Jack, 37n16

communism, 94

Corbett, Steve, 44, 87n6

covenant, Mosaic, blessings of (protection from enemies, blessing on the fruit of the womb, blessing on the fruit of the land), 17, 30, 30–34, 42; and obedience, 32–33; and the promise of God's presence, 31, 42; as a reversal of

Scripture Index

Short Studies in
Biblical Theology

This series is designed to help readers see the whole
Bible as a unified story—culminating in Jesus.

Insightful, accessible, and practical, these books
serve as bite-sized introductions to major
subjects in biblical theology.

Visit crossway.org/SSBT for more information.